PRESIDENTS AT WAR

HOW
GEORGE
WASHINGTON
FOUGHT THE
REVOLUTIONARY
WAR

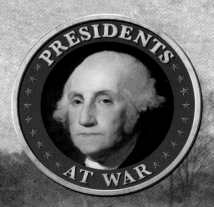

PRESIDENTS AT WAR

HOW GEORGE WASHINGTON FOUGHT THE REVOLUTIONARY WAR

Jeanne Nagle

Enslow Publishing
101 W. 23rd Street
Suite 240
New York, NY 10011
USA

enslow.com

Published in 2018 by Enslow Publishing, LLC.
101 W. 23rd Street, Suite 240, New York, NY 10011

Library of Congress Cataloging-in-Publication Data

Names: Nagle, Jeanne, author.

Title: How George Washington fought the Revolutionary War / Jeanne Nagle.

Description: New York : Enslow Publishing, 2018. | Series: Presidents at war
  | Includes bibliographical references and index. | Audience: Grades 7–12.

Identifiers: LCCN 2017004617 | ISBN 9780766085237 (library bound)

Subjects: LCSH: Washington, George, 1732–1799—Juvenile literature. |
  Presidents—United States—Biography—Juvenile literature. |
  Generals—United States—Biography—Juvenile literature. | United
  States—History—Revolution, 1775–1783—Juvenile literature.

Classification: LCC E312.66 .N34 2018 | DDC 973.4/1092 [B]—dc23

LC record available at https://lccn.loc.gov/2017004617

Printed in the United States of America

To Our Readers: We have done our best to make sure all website addresses in this book were active and appropriate when we went to press. However, the author and the publisher have no control over and assume no liability for the material available on those websites or on any websites they may link to. Any comments or suggestions can be sent by e-mail to customerservice@enslow.com.

★ CONTENTS ★

George Washington is known as the "father of our country." Even as a young man, Washington was a skilled horseman. This trait would serve him well in battles later in life.

INTRODUCTION

George Washington was a man of many talents. As a young man, he learned the necessary skills to become a surveyor, measuring and mapping parcels of land to determine the boundaries of ownership. After he inherited his stepbrother's estate—and purchased or otherwise earned hundreds of acres beyond that—he became a successful planter and gentleman farmer. From there, he segued into roles as a miller, exporter, and distiller of whiskey. Yet arguably the skills and attributes most associated with Washington revolve around his military prowess and political acumen—the latter was particularly evident during his two-term tenure as president of the United States.

Not surprisingly, the events of Washington's life influenced and informed what was to come on his path to renown. For instance, traversing the uncharted wilderness as a surveyor would later serve him well as he traveled and fought in the French and Indian War. Similarly, his experiences with Native American tribes during that conflict would prove useful while fighting the British during the American Revolution. Ably commanding first the Virginia militia and later the Continental Army prepared him to assume the mantle of leadership when he became the new nation's first political leader.

Unlike other US presidents, such as Abraham Lincoln and Franklin Delano Roosevelt, Washington did not serve as our nation's president during active wartime, since neither the presidency nor the country itself had been established during the French and Indian War or the American Revolution. Yet he did bring a certain level of political astuteness to his military dealings. Furthermore, his actions had a direct bearing on how each of these conflicts began, were waged, and ended. In the American Revolution, his leadership directly impacted the success of a group of rebels struggling to cast off the colonial manacles of Britain to stand as their own nation in charge of its own destiny.

Washington's political handling of matters of war was on display during other conflicts and uprisings that took place during his time in the new nation's highest office. His sending in army troops to settle a land dispute with British-backed Native American tribes and squelching the Whiskey Rebellion, both in 1794, reveal a man not afraid to use military might. His insistence on staying neutral in matters of foreign affairs, meanwhile, was a common theme throughout his presidency. Washington did not believe the United States was ready to enter into another war so soon after the revolution that had won the freshly formed nation its independence from Britain.

Washington also exhibited expertise in conflict resolution—although on a smaller scale than during a years-long war—by mediating disputes among his cabinet members.

Most famously, he was often forced to act as a referee between his secretary of state, Thomas Jefferson, and Alexander Hamilton, his secretary of the treasury. As president, he also fended off attacks on his own character, notably from Thomas Paine. It was a skill Washington grew adept at while in charge of the Continental Army, as detractors worked behind the scenes in an attempt to relieve him of his command.

WHERE IT BEGAN

The roots of George Washington's military career can be traced back to the future general and commander's teenage years. George was born on February 22, 1732. He was the eldest child of Augustine Washington and his second wife, Mary Ball Washington. (Mary and Augustine also had three more sons and a daughter.) Augustine was a successful tobacco planter and business owner in Virginia. He also was a land speculator, which is someone who buys land cheaply in the hope of selling it for more to make a profit.[1] Washington himself owned a lot of land, and Mary Ball Washington brought land with her to their marriage.[2]

Rather than wish to follow in his father's footsteps, young George wanted to be like Lawrence, his half brother from his father's first marriage. Lawrence was an officer in a colonial regiment who fought with the British in a war against Spain. He had sailed aboard the flagship of Admiral Edward Vernon and saw battle throughout the West Indies.[3] Upon his return from war, Lawrence continued his military career after being appointed adjutant general for the Northern Virginia militia. Adjutants were essentially the second in command of military units—in this case, colonial troops gathered to protect a specific portion of Virginia.

Portrait of Washington's older brother, Lawrence, who exerted a great deal of influence, directly and indirectly, over young George.

George greatly admired his brother. Early on, he was determined to make a similar life in the military, with its excitement and challenges, for himself.

Longing for Adventure

After his father died in 1743, George began spending a lot of time with Lawrence at the older brother's home on the Potomac River. The estate, formerly owned by Augustine and known as Little Hunting Creek, had been renamed Mount Vernon by Lawrence after his former military commander.

Knowing that his brother was keenly interested in a military career himself, Lawrence supposedly secured an appointment for fourteen-year-old George as a midshipman on a British navy ship. Whether Lawrence actually requested or got a commission for George, who was merely trying to enlist his brother's help in the matter, is unclear. Regardless, as noted in a letter to Lawrence from a neighbor of Mary Ball Washington, George's mother was totally against the idea from the start.[4] She forbid her boy from going to sea. He reluctantly gave in and the matter was dropped—at least for the time being.

Lawrence did eventually help his younger brother find work that would satisfy George's desire for adventure. Lawrence's wife, the former Anne Fairfax, came from a prominent family that owned millions of acres of land in Virginia. The Fairfax estate, Belvoir, was located only a few miles away from Mount Vernon. Family ties and neighboring estates brought young George to the attention of Ann's father, William, who acted as the agent for the Fairfax family land holdings. William needed surveyors

Washington's Assets

It may seem odd that George was considering a military commission at such a young age, but at the time it wasn't uncommon for young men to earn navy experience as a midshipman, or apprentice sailor, in the British Royal Navy. Besides, according to different accounts, he was unusually tall and strong for his age, and because of this he probably would have fared better onboard a ship than most other boys his age. Yet it is probably best that George would eventually become a soldier on land rather than at sea. He had developed keen riding skills as a boy and would come to be known for his excellent horsemanship.

to take measurements of an undeveloped portion of the Fairfax lands. In 1748, at the age of seventeen, George embarked on a month-long journey into an untamed section of western Virginia, known as the Northern Neck, as part of the surveyor team.

Wilderness Training

George's time in the Northern Neck wilderness with the Fairfax expedition was mostly on-the-job training. Although he did attend school until he was fifteen, his father's death left the family without enough funds to send George away to complete his education in England, as Lawrence and Augustine Jr. had done. Therefore, he received little to no formal training in a trade. Fortunately, he was able to pick up enough math and drawing skills, on his own and in association with William Fairfax's son George William, to show promise as a surveyor. The journey into Northern Neck, therefore, was his first professional position in that field.

Conditions during the trip were rough, to say the least. At that time, the Virginia frontier was uncharted territory. The land the surveyors were sent to survey was filled with overgrown vegetation and all sorts of creatures and bugs that could make life unpleasant, if not downright dangerous. George's journal detailing the expedition was filled with references to obstacles such as pouring rain, the raging currents of swollen rivers, muddy trails, treacherous mountain passes, and high winds that carried their tent away. The party even met up with a group of American Indians "coming from War with only one scalp," as he reported in his journal. In that same entry, he wrote that the surveyors shared alcohol with the natives, who then played music and danced around the campfire.[5]

Fruitful Employment

While his expedition into the Virginia frontier was not easy, and certainly not the most comfortable, George seems to have enjoyed the experience overall. Work as a surveyor gave him the opportunity to travel and even own land himself. The experience was not the same as being a soldier or a sailor, but it did have adventurous elements that appealed to the young man. Certainly interacting with various Native American tribes was exciting, while living off the land and dealing with the elements was challenging.

This is an artist's interpretation of Washington, the surveyor, in the field. Some of the tools that Washington used in his job as a surveyor had once belonged to his father, Augustine.

A year after returning from the Northern Neck, George was appointed as surveyor of Culpeper County in Virginia. Normally a seventeen-year-old would not be placed in such an important public service job, but having the influential William Fairfax, who had large land holdings in the

Washington the Writer

Much of what historians know about George Washington's teen and early adult years comes directly from the source. George avidly wrote in journals and letters sent to loved ones and commanding officers. His surveying trips and, later, his military excursions were dutifully recorded, and several of his surveys document his activities out in the field. One of his earliest known writing efforts was a list of etiquette guidelines titled *110 Rules of Civility & Decent Behaviour in Company and Conversation*. While these rules are believed to have been merely copied by a teenage George from an existing French work, they are of interest because the young man seemed to take them to heart. George used this guide as a way to better himself by applying these principles in his dealings with others.

county, to recommend him and act as a glowing reference went a long way toward securing him the position. The appointment marked George's entrance into the world of professional surveying.

At that time, Culpeper County was fairly well established—a far cry from the wilderness territories on which George had cut his surveying teeth. Frankly, there wasn't much land left that was unsettled and in need of surveying. With William Fairfax's knowledge and permission, he completed many surveys in Frederick County instead, which included a large percentage of land owned by the Fairfaxes.

Although he resigned his Culpeper position in 1750, George remained a professional surveyor and worked for two more years, usually in Frederick County.[6]

Losing Lawrence

By late 1751, George had other matters to occupy his time than surveying. Lawrence had become quite ill with tuberculosis, which he had contracted while sailing throughout the West Indies. Determining that the climate in Barbados, which was colonized by the British, would improve his health, he booked passage on a ship and set sail for the island. George went along as a traveling companion.

While abroad, George had the opportunity to dine and to speak with military personnel stationed on Barbados, as well as to tour the many forts and other defenses the British had established on the island. In a diary he kept during the trip, he noted that he was impressed with the protective show of force.[7]

Healthwise, the trip proved to be a bust for both brothers. Not only did Lawrence not get any better, but George contracted smallpox. In part because he was young and quite healthy before arriving in Barbados, George was able to recover from his illness before he returned home after spending six weeks on the island.

Lawrence did not accompany George back to Virginia, as he instead chose to travel on to Bermuda in an attempt to reverse the course of his tuberculosis. After several months there during the first half of 1752, he realized he was not getting better and decided to return to Mount Vernon. His health deteriorated quickly upon landing in Virginia, and within a month he was dead. George was devastated by the loss of his half brother.

Upon Lawrence's death, Mount Vernon went to his only surviving child, a daughter named Sarah. When the child died two years later, the property went to her mother. Anne was then living elsewhere with her second husband, George Lee, so she leased the estate to George.

George the Adjutant

Mount Vernon was not the only reminder of Lawrence that George hoped to enjoy. With his interest in the military rejuvenated by his trip to Barbados, the younger brother actively sought to take over the adjutant position Lawrence formerly held. While sometimes this type of position could be inherited from a family member, it would have been unusual for it to be given to, or won by, someone who did not have military experience.[8]

But as was the case when he was appointed surveyor of Culpeper County, George was the beneficiary of influential people interceding on his behalf. Virginia Governor Robert Dinwiddie bestowed the rank of major on George and named him an adjutant. It was not the position George had requested, overseeing the militia in the Northern Neck, but instead he was granted the adjutancy of a district to the south.

In his newly acquired position, George was responsible for overseeing the training and readiness of militia foot soldiers in one of four military districts within the Virginia colony. Colonial militias were made up of part-time volunteer troops that, when the land was first colonized,

Washington is shown in his Virginia militia uniform. He began his military career as an adjutant and worked his way up to the rank of lieutenant colonel.

were meant to protect their citizens from attacks by Native Americans. Later, they were something of a "law and order" force within their colonies or districts.[9] They could be pressed into service abroad, as Lawrence had been, when reinforcements were needed by the British regular army. Many militia soldiers came from a lower-class upbringing. In order to make them proper representatives of the king's forces, they were trained to be more genteel, or well mannered. That task fell to adjutants such as George. He was also responsible for making sure the troops from his district knew how to use their weapons and that they were ready and willing to follow orders.

A Point of Conflict

George's appointment to adjutant could not have come at a better time for a young man looking to make his mark. Tensions were once again brewing between longtime rivals Britain and France over who could rightfully claim ownership to certain parts of North America. At stake were not only settlement rights but lucrative trading rights, as well. The British had established thirteen colonies along the eastern seaboard and claimed the land between French-controlled Canada and Spanish-controlled Florida across the width of the continent. The French, meanwhile, claimed a swath of territory roughly from the Great Lakes down through the Mississippi River basin by virtue of having sent explorers southward from Canada beginning in the 1680s.

A particular point of contention in this simmering imperial feud was a section of land known as the Ohio Country. British traders from Pennsylvania and, especially, Virginia who had moved westward and settled in this area

This is a map of the Western frontier of the United States, circa 1785. Toward the bottom right is the Ohio River Valley, which was hotly contested in the French and Indian War.

came under attack from French forces starting in 1750. Furthermore, the French began forcibly removing British traders and settlers from the Ohio Country and building forts to protect land they deemed as theirs.

In 1753, acting on advice from the crown, Virginia's Lieutenant Governor Robert Dinwiddie sent a messenger to French forces reasserting that the land in question belonged to Great Britain and that the French should abandon their forts and negate their claims to the area immediately. The governor put out a call for volunteers to take his message to the French. Twenty-one-year-old George Washington answered that call. For his service he was commissioned as a major in the British army, which must have greatly pleased the young man who had, for so long, desired a military career.

A FIRST TASTE OF BATTLE

In October 1753, George Washington set out to deliver Governor Dinwiddie's demand that the French leave the Ohio Country and revoke all claims to the land going forward. On the journey with him were six men: French interpreter Jacob Van Braam; Christopher Gist as a pilot, or guide; and four others who were Indian traders and frontiersmen.[1] While it was true that Washington had little military experience at that point, Dinwiddie trusted him to succeed at this mission for a number of reasons. First, he was the brother of Lawrence Washington, who had acquitted himself well as an adjutant before his death. Second, he had the admiration and backing of the prominent Fairfax family. Finally, Washington's experience as a surveyor proved he was able to tackle whatever the wilderness could throw at him.[2]

That last point would prove to be very important. Washington and his crew set out on their mission late in the fall, when the impending winter would turn the elements against them. As had occurred during his first surveyor trip in the Northern Neck, Washington ran into foul weather, including heavy rains and plentiful snowfall. Travel was difficult in these conditions and caused delays in Washington's travel schedule throughout his journey.

Ulterior Motives

As he traveled through the Ohio Country, Washington was told to scout stretches of land that could be used to build British forts. Of particular interest was a location where the Monongahela and Allegheny rivers meet and feed into the Ohio River, known as the Forks of Ohio. (This area would later become the city of Pittsburgh.) A fort placed at this spot would be well protected because of the surrounding terrain and would have ready access to waterways leading to British settlements in the area.

He also was on the lookout for land that could be purchased by the Ohio Company of Virginia, a trade and land speculation organization founded in part by Lawrence and George William Fairfax, the son of Washington's primary benefactor. Dinwiddie was also a member of the organization. Washington hoped to help representatives of the Ohio Company gain control of large tracts of the territory to further their settlement and trading endeavors.

About a month after leaving Virginia, Washington and his group arrived at a Native American settlement and trading post known as Logstown. He hoped to win the favor and trust of certain native tribes in the area, as the Indians could prove to be powerful allies between the British and the French. But because they had been living in the area before any Europeans came to North America, the American Indians felt the contested land was theirs and that they

Washington and his guide, Christopher Gist, shown crossing the icy Allegheny River on the journey to meet with the French at Fort LeBoeuf.

were owed something for letting the French and British settle and trade in the area. Aware of this, Washington came bearing gifts, which he presented to a representative of Tanacharison, the leader of the Mingo Native American tribe who was known simply as Half-King. "I gave him a String of Wampum and a Twist of Tobacco," Washington wrote in his journal.[3]

He further reported that his meeting with Tanacharison went so well that Half-King provided Washington's men with an escort to Fort LeBoeuf.

On to Fort LeBoeuf

From Logstown, the party traveled some seventy miles, through more horrible weather, to the Indian town of Venango. There they met with French army officers, who cordially invited the Virginians to dine with them. As Washington related in his journal:

> The Wine, as they dosed themselves pretty plentifully with it, soon banished the Restraint which at first appeared in their Conversation; and gave a Licence to their Tongues to reveal their Sentiments more freely. They told me That it was their absolute Design to take Possession of the Ohio, and by G__ they would do it.[4]

Finally, on December 11, Washington and his party reached their target, Fort LeBoeuf, which was situated between Lake Erie and French Creek. Washington was unable to meet with the fort's commander, Jacques Legardeur de Saint-Pierre, until the next day. When the two did meet, Washington gave Saint-Pierre a letter outlining Governor Dinwiddie's demands, which the French commander wanted to be translated and discussed in private with other officers at the fort.

While he was waiting for Saint-Pierre's official answer, Washington had several conversations with him and other officers at the fort. The French at Fort LeBoeuf were as defiant as those men Washington had encountered at

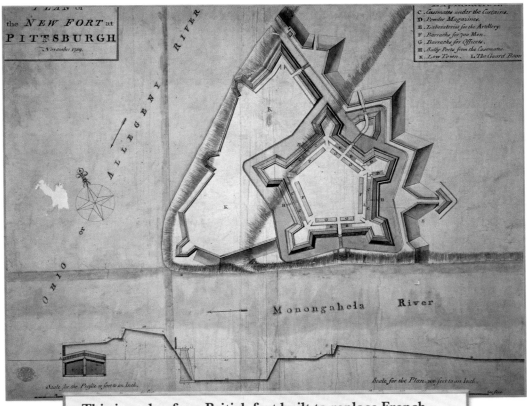

This is a plan for a British fort built to replace French Fort Duquesne in 1759. On his way to Fort LeBoeuf, Washington scouted out places for British forts to be built.

Venango. Many residents of the fort stated flat-out that the French had no intention of abandoning their series of forts and leaving the Ohio Country. Furthermore, Saint-Pierre defended the rights of the French to take a number of English traders from the area up to Canada as prisoners.

Finally, three days after he had arrived at Fort LeBoeuf, Washington received a sealed letter from Saint-Pierre as an official reply to Dinwiddie. The Virginians wasted no

Washington the Spy

While he was waiting for the French response to Dinwiddie's proclamation, Washington was secretly completing another mission, the terms of which had been disclosed to him off the record. The young major was told to gather as much information as he could about the French in the area—from the number of troops to details about their forts and other fortifications.

Washington made notes of what he saw and heard in his travel journal during the entire trip. He asked the Native Americans with whom he stayed, while working on an alliance, what they knew about French activity in the Ohio Country. He casually pumped the French officers at Venango for information over dinner and drinks. Washington also made a point of listening in on conversations at Fort LeBoeuf. Because he was kept waiting by Saint-Pierre and his men, he was able to gather quite a bit of information about life at this fort through careful listening and observation. All the intelligence he gathered was compiled and reported back to Governor Dinwiddie upon Washington's return to Virginia.

time in taking their leave of the French, and they began the difficult journey home.

From Messenger to Leader

The French reply to Dinwiddie's order to leave the area was probably not unexpected, but it was definitely unwelcome. Their insistence that the Ohio Country was theirs was basically an invitation for the British to respond with force if they wanted to make good on their own claim to the territory.

Shortly after Washington delivered the bad news, Dinwiddie swung into action by requesting that Virginia militia forces be sent to the Ohio Country to engage the French. When that plan failed because volunteer militiamen did not answer the call, the governor instead sought funding from the Crown to gather a regiment of men to act as an army. No doubt the promise of land from the region, if they were victorious, drew many volunteers to join the regiment. Washington was promoted from major to lieutenant colonel, and in March 1754, he started on a return trip to the Ohio Country. This time he was second in command and leader of the newly formed army unit. His superior, Colonel Joshua Fry, remained in Virginia in an attempt to recruit more men to the cause.[5]

During his journey back into the wilderness, Washington got word that the French had put a stop to the building of a British fort at the Forks—the highly strategic location he had scouted for the British when he traveled to Fort LeBoeuf months earlier—and were at the site trying to build a fort of their own. Reconnaissance indicated that French forces there outnumbered the Virginia army's men by about ten to one. Washington had his men hunker down in an area south of the Forks called the Great Meadows to wait for reinforcements to stage an attack on the French fort under construction.

Before more soldiers could arrive, however, he received word from his Native American ally Tanacharison that a small party of French soldiers was camped not far from their position. Instead of staying put and following Dinwiddie's orders to fight only if attacked, Washington decided to lead about half of his regiment and a portion of Tanacharison's warriors to where the French party was encamped. Little did he know that this decision would be the spark that started the fires of war.

Incident at Jumonville Glen

The group traveled under the cover of night and reached the French camp in a small glen the next morning, May 28. Soon the glen was surrounded with the Mingo warriors in position behind the Frenchmen and the Virginia army squad facing the front. Washington ordered his troops to slowly advance on the Frenchmen, who were led by the French-Canadian officer Joseph Coulon de Jumonville.

What happened next remains something of a mystery to this day. The French claimed that they were attacked outright when the Virginians came at them firing the first shots. While admitting his decision to confront the encamped Frenchmen, Washington claimed that French forces began the fight and that his troops were only defending themselves per Dinwiddie's orders. No matter who started it, the skirmish ended with Coulon de Jumonville and nearly half of the small French party dead and several more wounded; only a few French soldiers had managed to escape. Many of the remaining wounded were killed after the battle had ended. Washington claimed Tanacharison's men killed and scalped the survivors, while Half-King blamed the Virginians, who got carried away in the heat of battle.[6]

The attack at what became known as Jumonville Glen heightened existing tensions between the French and the British so strongly that it is widely considered the start of the French and Indian War, which was not officially declared until the following year. (Beginning in 1756 and ending in 1763, the war was known as the Seven Years War in Europe.) The Jumonville incident also caused major problems for Washington. For one thing, he had disobeyed orders and overstepped his bounds by making decisions that rightly should have been made by his superior, Colonel Fry. Making matters worse, some sources reported Coulon de Jumonville had been on a diplomatic mission to deliver a message to Washington. The parallels to Washington's own situation the year before at Fort LeBoeuf were striking.[7]

Perhaps the most immediate dilemma was that the French, soon informed about the incident at the glen by those who had escaped, would be duty bound to respond to the attack with a show of force of their own. French troops in the Ohio Country far outnumbered Washington's men, even considering Tanacharison's warriors. Washington and his small band of men returned to the camp at the Great Meadows. To protect himself and his men, the lieutenant colonel immediately gave the order to build a fort on the campsite, which he named Fort Necessity.

❝The volley fired by a young Virginian in the backwoods of America set the world on fire.❞

—British author Horace Walpole

A color illustration of the mortal wounding of Coulon de Jumonville at the glen that now bears his name. Washington led militia forces in the attack.

By all accounts, Fort Necessity was not much of a fort. It was built very quickly and was actually a barricade made of hastily carved logs standing on end in a simple circle.[8] The land on which the wall was built had turned to a swampy mess, courtesy of the rain that seemed to fall every day. Flooding was a problem in the trenches outside the barricade and within the compound itself.

Forced to Surrender

While erecting the fort, Washington received word that the regiment's commanding officer, Colonel Fry, had died after falling from his horse while on his way to join the troops at the Great Meadows. Fry's death meant Washington was now the commander of the Virginia army. He received a field promotion to the rank of colonel. Shortly after work on the fort was completed, the men who had been directly under Fry's command joined the Virginia regiment, as did a company of British regulars, as officially commissioned British soldiers were called from South Carolina under the command of Captain James McKay.

A little more than a month after the skirmish at Jumonville Glen, French forces had tracked Washington and his men to the Great Meadows and Fort Necessity. The French soldiers, joined by allied Indian warriors, numbered more than seven hundred, and they came at the Virginians in full force starting on the morning of July 3, 1754. By the end of the day, the Virginia regiment had lost more than one hundred men, and many more were wounded or dying. Out of food and unable to use what gunpowder they had left because it had gotten wet in the constant downpour, Washington and McKay were forced to surrender.

The British and colonial commanders met the next morning with the French commander, who, coincidentally, was the half brother of Coulon de Jumonville. The terms of surrender were that Washington would sign a document stating he had "assassinated" the French commander at the glen in cold blood. In return, Washington and the remainder of his men were allowed to return to Virginia instead of being taken as prisoners.

In another coincidence that would seem significant decades later, Washington signed the documents of surrender at Fort Necessity on the fourth of July.

AT WAR AND AT HOME

Despite having surrendered what was technically a British fort and admitting—at least on paper—that he had murdered a French emissary, Washington did not return to Virginia discouraged. On the contrary, he seems to have been invigorated by his first battle experience. In a letter home after the attack at Jumonville Glen, Washington wrote of the experience, "I heard the bullets whistle, and, believe me there is something charming in the sound."[1]

What he did not find so charming was the way colonial officers were treated. Troops raised in the colonies in were in no way considered the equal of their British regular counterparts. No doubt spurred by the rough conditions faced by the Virginia Regiment, Washington had written to Dinwiddie from the field complaining about a lack of junior officers in the regiment, as well as general assistance from the governor's office. He further noted that the Virginia army's officers had to do hard work for very little pay. Lieutenant Governor Dinwiddie's response to Washington's pay complaint was along the lines of "You should have thought of that before you accepted your commission."

A Brief Intermission

With Colonel Fry gone, Dinwiddie needed to appoint an officer from the British regular ranks as commander of the Virginia Regiment. Colonel James Innes was first appointed to lead the colonial troops back into the Ohio Country, followed by Maryland's governor, Horatio Sharp, who had been named commander in chief of operations to secure the Forks and the surrounding region. This left an already disgruntled Washington once again second in command of the troops.

When neither Innes nor Sharp seemed to make much headway toward their assigned goal, Dinwiddie felt the need to take drastic action. He disbanded the Virginia Regiment and broke the troops into smaller companies in which no man should rise beyond the rank of captain. If Washington was to stay with one of the Virginia companies, he would have to suffer a demotion. Instead, in October 1754, he decided to resign from his commission and leave the military. He would spend the next five months as a planter working the land of Mount Vernon, which he was leasing from Lawrence's widow, Anne.

Washington had walked away from a life in the service to protest what he considered to be unfair treatment. Yet he still longed to be a soldier remembered for stunning victories rather than his defeat at Fort Necessity. Fortunately, he was offered a chance to redeem himself not long after resigning his commission.

In his absence, fighting between British and French troops over claims to the Ohio Country had continued. In particular, the British had redoubled their efforts to capture Fort Duquesne, the French fort that had been built at the

Forks. The Crown had sent career officer Major General Edward Braddock to the Americas to serve as commander in chief of all British forces there. Braddock took it upon himself to lead the charge against the fort at the Forks, and he asked Washington—who had informally surveyed the area two years earlier during his first mission into the Ohio Country—to join him as a civilian volunteer aide.[2] Anxious to return to battle, Washington accepted Braddock's offer.

Warriors at Odds

Washington accepted the job of Braddock's aide-de-camp in part because he wanted to learn how British regular officers handled their troops. Unfortunately, his view of Braddock as a military mentor appears to have dimmed over the course of the few months he spent under the major general's command.

Braddock was an older soldier and set in his ways. Even though he asked Washington to be his aide because of his knowledge of the Ohio Country and experience in dealing with the French, he often had trouble heeding the latter's advice. Washington mentioned in a letter to William Fairfax, dated June 7, 1775, that he and Braddock had frequent, heated arguments and that the general never backed down from his point of view, "let it ever be so incompatible with reason or common sense."

Apparently Washington also did not care for the general's opinion of the colonies themselves. As he wrote in that same letter, Braddock "... looks upon the country, I believe, as void of honour and honesty."[3]

GEN. BRADDOCK.

This portrait shows Major General Edward Braddock, the commander of the British forces. Washington resumed his paused military career as an aide to Braddock.

Battle of the Monongahela

Setting out in April, Braddock led his large force of men toward the Ohio Country using a long section of the route carved through the wilderness by Washington's Virginia militia in 1753. When the troops came to the Great Meadows and the broken remains of Fort Necessity, Braddock began blazing a new trail to accommodate the large number of troops and heavy artillery, such as cannons, that he brought with him from Britain. But that proved too time-consuming, so he decided to take Washington's advice and march his men, with only a few artillery pieces, across the mountains toward the Monongahela River.[4] His second in command, Colonel Thomas Dunbar, was ordered to follow with the bulk of the artillery. The two planned to meet up before attacking Fort Duquesne.

Unfortunately for Braddock and his men, those plans were quickly derailed. Soon after the combined British and colonial troops had crossed the Monongahela on July 9, they found themselves under attack. The French and their Native American allies lashed out at them from the cover of the surrounding forest. Panicked, the British-led troops were thrown into such disarray that Braddock could not pull them back together into an efficient fighting force.

After three hours of fierce fighting, the smoke of battle cleared enough for the British and colonial forces to take stock of their situation. The toll on their side was enormous, with nearly two-thirds of their men dead or wounded. Washington's impressions of the carnage were quite different than the euphoria he expressed after Jumonville Glen. Gone was mention of the "charming" sound of flying bullets, and it was replaced by "the groans,

Washington (*right, astride his horse*) picked up the slack created by the wounding of Braddock during the Battle of the Monongahela.

lamentations, and crys ... of the wounded for help," which he wrote "were enough to pierce a heart of adamant."[5]

Among the casualties was Braddock himself. At great risk, Washington carried his commander off the battlefield and out of harm's way. Legend has it that Washington came away from the fighting with bullet holes piercing his hat and clothing but his body unharmed. With Braddock dead and many other officers killed or incapacitated, Washington took charge and ordered the troops to retreat. After burying Braddock, the colonial and British regular troops made it back to their camp at the Great Meadows.

Striking a Deal

After the disastrous Battle of the Monongahela, Washington's reputation as a brave soldier grew as the colonists' opinion of the British regular forces sank. Once again, Lieutenant Governor Dinwiddie reorganized the Virginia Army, without the addition of British forces, and he asked Washington to come back as the commander with the rank of colonel.

For his part, Washington had some demands. He wanted money set aside to pay expenses and the ability to choose his own officers, thus addressing his original complaints directed at Dinwiddie prior to the incident at Jumonville Glen.[6] Dinwiddie agreed to these conditions, but another of Washington's requests—to receive a royal commission as a British army officer—was out of his control.

By May 1756, Britain had formally declared war against France and the country's Native American allies. The Virginia Army under Washington was assigned to protect British citizens, whether they were colonists, settlers, or traders, on the colony's frontier. Washington spent a good portion of his first year as regiment commander away from his troops and the battle lines. When he wasn't fighting the bureaucracy at regimental headquarters, he was traveling around Virginia trying to recruit troops or secure rations for his men. He was known as a tough disciplinarian who worked hard for his troops and expected absolute loyalty in return. He was reportedly not above having soldiers publicly flogged or beaten if they stepped out of line. He seemed to have saved his special wrath for deserters.[7]

Selective Service

Washington's attempts to recruit soldiers for the "new and improved" Virginia Army ran into a huge snag in the form of draft restrictions. He felt that, as written, rules governing the colonial militia put the burden on poor families, whose sons overwhelmingly represented the rank-and-file troops within the Virginia Army. Members of the upper classes seemed to get a pass when it came to serving in the military. Washington pleaded his case before the Virginia House of Burgesses, or legislature, to no avail.

There also was a problem with militiamen deserting once they had joined, or were drafted into, the army. Rounding up deserters was a difficult task made tougher when colonists, angered by Virginia's participation in a war between the British and the French, helped soldiers evade those who would have them return to service.[8] Is it any wonder that Washington spent the last six months of 1755 simply trying to find and retain militia recruits?

Second Resignation

In the fall of 1758, Washington and his men took part in a mission to apprehend enemy raiders who attacked British horses and livestock at a supply depot within the Ohio Country. The Virginians captured two enemy soldiers who revealed that Fort Duquesne was only lightly guarded

British forces and their Native American allies watch as Fort Duquesne burns to the ground. The French sabotaged the fort as the British approached.

and was ripe for an attack. This came as excellent news to Washington's superior, Brigadier General John Forbes, who had been tasked with capturing the fort.

But before the British could capture it, the French left their barricade and detonated explosives that reduced the fort to rubble. Even though there was no fort left standing, the result was the same—the French had been driven from the Forks. Washington, who had begun his career as a military commander with a campaign to regain the Forks location for a British fort, must have felt as if he had come full circle. He once again resigned his commission and set his sights on returning to Mount Vernon to become a full-time planter and farmer.

PRELUDE TO A REVOLUTION

For someone who had his heart set on a military career and had achieved a modicum of success on the battlefield, Washington seemed to adjust to life outside of soldiering fairly well and fairly quickly. He approached his role of estate owner and planter with the same gusto he brought to his military endeavors. He made Mount Vernon a successful planting operation, which made him a respected and wealthy individual.

In truth, Washington's transition from soldier to civilian had started before he resigned his military commission for a second time. Perhaps disappointed with the outcome each time he petitioned the House of Burgesses, first on behalf of his troops and then on his quest to be awarded a royal commission, Washington had run a successful campaign in 1758 to join the legislative body. Another important and life-changing occurrence happened that year, as well. He had met and become engaged to the wealthy widow Martha Dandridge Custis.

The colonies were also undergoing some changes during this time. Their relationship with Britain, already strained because of their second-class, subservient status over the course of a war fought on their land, was reaching a breaking point. A revolution seemed imminent.

Gentleman Farmer

Washington had not spent any extended amount of time at Mount Vernon, the estate he leased from Lawrence's widow, since he rejoined the army as Braddock's aide in 1755. By the time Washington was ready to settle on the estate and begin his life as a farmer, the main house that Lawrence had built was in need of repair. He got right to work soon after

The life of a gentleman farmer at Mount Vernon seemed to suit Washington well—at least for a while. The farmhands in this image are some of the slaves Washington owned.

Washington's Slaves

Slavery was commonplace in colonial Virginia. Considered property, slaves were routinely bought and sold by planters and rich property owners, and many slaves were even willed to inheritors after a death. For instance, when Washington was eleven years old, his father left him an inheritance that included his property at Ferry Farm and ten slaves. An additional eighteen slaves were his, considered part and parcel of the property, when he officially inherited Mount Vernon upon Anne's death in 1761.

Washington gained even more "human property" when he married Martha Dandridge Custis, a wealthy widow who had inherited some eighty slaves upon the death of her first husband. There are also records of Washington purchasing additional slaves to work in his fields and in the main house at Mount Vernon.

By the end of his life, Washington had a change of heart about slavery. In his will, he directed that the more than three hundred people enslaved at Mount Vernon and his other properties be freed upon the death of his wife.

arriving back home in 1758 by overseeing not only repairs but also improvements to the house. The latter included adding a second floor to the existing structure.

Washington had grown up on Ferry Farm, one of his father's plantation holdings, so he was familiar with planting and growing, although not as the lord and master of an estate. When it came to making Mount Vernon a profitable enterprise, he used a tried-and-true approach—

studying. Much as he had when he began his surveying career, he "took to the books" to learn the latest agricultural techniques. He put into practice what he had learned, oversaw the slaves and others who worked his fields, and even contributed physical labor of his own.

When Washington first started planting at Mount Vernon, tobacco was his cash crop, meaning it was his main source of revenue. However, study and experience taught him that tobacco damaged the land by sucking all the nutrients out of the soil over time and leaving the acreage unproductive. Instead, he began to plant different crops, particularly wheat, in its place.[1]

Land purchases, which began when Washington had worked as a surveyor, gradually bumped up Mount Vernon's original 2,500 acres enough to make it quite the respectable estate. Eventually, Washington's holdings at Mount Vernon grew to 8,000 acres, which was divided into five individual farms: River, Muddy Hole, Dogue, Union, and the Mansion House Farm. The last was a farm in name only. The grounds of the house were landscaped, not cultivated.[2]

George and Martha

On a trip to Williamsburg in 1758, Colonel Washington met twenty-seven-year-old Martha Dandridge Custis, a widow with two children: Jacky, who was four years old, and Patsy, who was two years old. He called upon Martha, meaning he visited her at her home, twice that March, and within a matter of months, the pair were engaged. They were married on January 6, 1759. The ceremony took place at Martha's inherited estate, White House Plantation.

This is a portrait of Martha Dandridge Custis, who married Washington in 1759.

Some cynics believe that Washington was drawn to Martha because she was wealthy and could offer him land and status. And it was true that she brought much to the marriage, including 17,500 acres of land and nearly three hundred slaves. She, it has been claimed, was tired of running her late husband's business affairs and was on the lookout for a husband who could take over the running of her estate. The less hardened think that while these issues may have played a part in bringing these two souls together, George and Martha Washington actually had a mutual admiration and affection for each other.

Written evidence seems to support the latter theory. In a letter to Martha, dated July 20, 1758, while he was on the march with General Forbes into the Ohio Country, Washington wrote:

> A courier is starting for Williamsburg, and I embrace the opportunity to send a few words to one whose life is now inseparable from mine. Since that happy hour when we made our pledges to each other, my thoughts have been continually going to you as another Self.

Two months later, in a letter to George William Fairfax's wife, he put the case more simply: "'Tis true, I profess myself a votary of love."[3]

❝I believe I have settled with an amiable wife for the rest of my life and hope to find in my retirement more happiness than I have ever found in a large and troubled world.❞

When he married Martha, Washington also became an instant parent to his stepchildren. By all accounts, he loved Jacky and Patsy as if they were his own. He liked to lavish them with gifts, some imported from London, and prepared for their futures by assiduously overseeing their inheritance.[4] He and Martha did not have any children of their own, but Washington felt fulfilled as a parent because of the Custis children and, later, as a grandfather to Jacky's offspring.

House of Burgesses

In April 1759, George, Martha, and the children settled into a comfortable life at Mount Vernon after spending the first three months of the couple's marriage at White House Plantation in Williamsburg. Washington also took a trip to the capital in February of that year to fulfill his duties as a newly elected member of the House of Burgesses, which met twice a year for anywhere from two weeks to a month at a time.[5] Once again, Washington had followed in Lawrence's footsteps by winning a seat in the Virginia legislature.

As a precursor to today's US Congress, it makes sense that there are certain similarities between the Virginia House of Burgesses and the US legislative body in form and function. There were 106 seats in the House, composed of two for each county and one each for Jamestown, Williamsburg, Norfolk, and the influential College of William and Mary.[6] In 1758, Washington ran as a candidate from Frederick County. One burgess, as the representatives were called, who was referred to as the speaker, presided over all legislative meetings. Burgesses also served on various committees that oversaw the writing of certain bills or attending to other legislative business, such as listening to the petitions of constituents from their town or county. One of the committees on which Washington served when he was first elected reviewed claims made by French and Indian War veterans.[7]

The Virginia House of Burgesses was composed of wealthy men who owned quite a bit of land and consequently held special status within their communities.

Casting a Vote

The election process for the House of Burgesses was quite different from what most Americans experience today. Elections were held at the will of the governor, usually every two to four years, but there could be no gap between elections longer than seven years. Instead of casting ballots, people cast voice votes, where they proclaimed in front of an audience the name of their candidate of choice. County sheriffs recorded and tallied the votes. The top two vote recipients from each county were declared the winners.

Voters had to be at least twenty-one years old. Additionally, there were rules governing who was eligible to vote tied to how much land a person owned. Therefore, those proclaiming their votes were wealthy white men. Landholders could vote in any county in which they held enough land, but they could only vote for one candidate in each location.

Washington's election, then, could be considered a confirmation that he had achieved his goal of becoming a respectable man of consequence.

Washington's first term as a burgess lasted until 1761, when he was elected to the House yet again, but this time it was for Fairfax County. It was this seat that he would keep through subsequent elections until 1775—when Virginia royal Governor John Murray, earl of Dunmore, dissolved the legislative body in response to protests and insurrection on the part of the colonies.

Acting Up

Until the early 1760s, the British government had given the North American colonies a certain measure of independence in regard to the handling of internal affairs, provided they remained loyal to the Crown. For instance, the colonies could govern themselves through assemblies such as the House of Burgesses as long as the directives, decisions, and laws of these legislatures did not conflict with British law or dictates. Colonists had also historically benefited from light and somewhat sporadic enforcement of British trade regulations. But the British victory in the French and Indian War changed all that.

As a result of the 1763 Treaty of Paris, which ended the French and Indian War, Britain had added substantial landholdings to its empire, including the Ohio Country and parts of Canada in North America. Neither waging war nor empire building comes cheap, however; the British government soon found itself in dire need of additional revenue in order to effectively settle and govern its vast holdings around the world. One solution was to impose taxes on goods sent to the colonies and manipulate trade regulations to the Crown's advantage.

In 1764, British Parliament passed the Sugar Act, which made it costlier for the colonies to import sugar and molasses from non-British producers. Furthermore, the act strengthened the penalties for not paying duties, or taxes, on these and other imports through smuggling. These moves were designed to give plantations in the British West Indies a monopoly on colonial sugar and molasses imports and thereby raise revenue. These measures did not please the colonists, and it was about to get worse.

In order to cut costs associated with having British regulars stationed in North America, Parliament passed the Quartering Act the following year. This put the burden of feeding, housing, and transporting British protective troops on the colonies, and it also meant colonial merchants no longer received the income from British payment for these services.

Parliament then passed the Stamp Act in 1766. Virtually every important piece of paper—legal documents, newspapers, periodicals, and pamphlets, among others—was required to bear an ink stamp purchased from the British government.

Next, the colonies had to suffer four laws known as the Townshend Acts. Three of these acts raised taxes on imported British goods, created stricter rules regarding the collection of import duties, and allowed British tea to be exported to North America without being taxed. The fourth act allowed Parliament to suspend the New York Assembly until it was in compliance with the Quartering Act.

Acting Out

As the number of repressive acts grew, so did colonial resentment. The revenue-producing measures imposed by Britain during this time frame gave rise to acts of rebellion. For example, in March of 1770, opposition to the Townshend Acts led to a deadly clash between British soldiers and colonists known as the Boston Massacre. Perhaps the most famous of these rebellions was the Boston Tea Party in 1773. Colonial retaliation, coupled with less than desirable revenue gains, sometimes resulted in certain acts being repealed. For instance, the Stamp Act was repealed in 1770, and the Townshend Acts were repealed in 1770—except the British tea tax exemption. Overall, however, the systematic imposition of laws and high taxes remained intact.

Sometimes Parliament even added new restrictions as punishment for colonial refusal to abide by earlier acts. In response to the Boston Tea Party, the British approved what was known in the colonies as the Intolerable Acts in 1774. The acts closed the port of Boston, changed the Massachusetts charter to restrict the province's right to self-govern, and allowed British officials accused of wrongdoing to stand trial in the relative safety of the British courts. They also strengthened and expanded parts of the Quartering Act within the city of Boston. British officials had hoped that the Intolerable Acts would serve as a warning to other colonies to either submit or suffer the same consequences. Instead, they served to bring all the colonies together in a bold act of unified defiance.

As a member of the House of Burgesses, Washington was on the front lines when it came to Virginia's response to what many saw as British tyranny. He opposed the Stamp

This drawing, made by Paul Revere circa 1779, shows the fighting between British regulars and colonists that became known as the Boston Massacre.

Act and was supposedly the first to sign an official protest document against taxation measures of the Townshend Acts.[8] But in 1774, once the Intolerable Acts were enacted and Governor Murray dissolved the House of Burgesses, Washington and his fellow resisters, called patriots, knew the time for serious action had come.

Meeting of the Continental Congress

On September 4, 1774, delegates from twelve of the thirteen colonies (Georgia was the lone holdout) met in Philadelphia, Pennsylvania, to craft a response to Britain's heavy-handed and intrusive governance of the colonies. This gathering, which was considered an extension of all the individual colonial assemblies rolled into one, was called the Continental Congress. Among their number were several prominent statesmen and patriots, including Patrick Henry, John Adams, Samuel Adams, John Jay, and, of course, George Washington. In this session of their meeting, the delegates drafted a letter to King George III stating their collective displeasure over the Intolerable Acts and threatening a boycott of British goods if the act was not repealed. The group agreed to meet again in the spring of 1775 if their concerns and demands were ignored.

Between the first meeting of the Continental Congress and the proposed second meeting, the conflict between Britain and the colonies went from the passing of acts and the sending of letters to physical confrontation. On the night of April 18, 1775, British troops had been sent to the town of Lexington, Massachusetts, to arrest rebellion leaders Samuel Adams and John Hancock for treason. The two patriots had been tipped off that their arrest was imminent and had left town. In their place, the British troops encountered a group of armed militiamen on the town's common. When the militiamen refused to back down, the British opened fire, which resulted in eight dead and ten wounded.

From there, the troops marched on nearby Concord, where it was rumored the rebels had stockpiled weapons and supplies. Arriving in Concord the next morning, the British came face to face with another band of militiamen crossing the Old North Bridge over the Concord River. Fighting again broke out between the two sides, but this time the British sounded a retreat and fled back to Boston.

In a letter to George William Fairfax, dated May 31, 1775, Washington commented on the battles of Lexington and Concord by stating that "the once happy and peaceful plains of America are either to be drenched with blood, or Inhabited by Slaves."[9] A second meeting of the Continental Congress could not be avoided. Once again, Washington set out for Philadelphia to set a course of action for the beleaguered colonies.

THE BATTLE FOR INDEPENDENCE BEGINS

It was, by and large, the opinion of the colonists that Britain had declared war by opening fire on colonial troops at Lexington and Concord. There could no longer be any hope of a reconciliation with the Crown. With that topic off the agenda, the Second Continental Congress went straight to addressing matters of battle readiness and how the separate colonies would best come together to operate, militarily and politically, as a united front.

The delegates were divided into committees charged with debating various issues. They would then report their findings back to the group at large for a deciding vote. No doubt because of his well-known experience as a leader during the French and Indian War, Washington was placed on the committee that discussed battle preparedness and other military matters.[1]

One of the issues at hand was how to build a strong, successful army that could beat the British regulars at their own game. There was a growing movement underway to make raising an army the responsibility of the Continental Congress. It seemed a fair way to combine the forces of the thirteen different militias without putting too much burden on, or ascribing too much power to, any one colonial army and its officers. The measure to create a Continental Army was passed by vote of the assembled delegates on June 14, 1775.

Commander in Chief

The question now before the Congress was who should lead the army. Soon after the vote on whether or not to centralize the military had been completed, John Adams nominated Washington as commander of the newly formed Continental Army. Historians suggest that Washington was eager to be appointed to the post. They point to his desire for a military career from an early age, his many attempts to secure a royal commission, and the qualifying circumstances surrounding his two resignations. The fact that he had a "buff and blue" uniform made for himself—which he reportedly wore every day of the Second Continental Congress—might have been a pretty good tip-off about his willingness to serve, as well.[2] Liked and respected by the other delegates, who at this session included fellow Virginian Thomas Jefferson, Washington was elected to the leadership post unanimously.

❝ [A]s the Congress desires, I will enter upon the momentous duty, and exert every power I possess in their service, and for the support of the glorious cause.❞

This portrait of General George Washington shows him wearing his now-famous "blue and buff" uniform. The uniform and its color scheme were copied by some colonial companies.

Washington took his orders from what was now simply called Congress, and he was required to stay in contact with congressional leaders. Other than abiding by the Articles of War, which Congress had drafted in about a week, he was given almost free rein about how to handle engagement with the enemy in the field of battle and could appoint his own officers. Likewise, he was given the power to deal with any American citizen who chose to side and fight with the British as he saw fit—as long as he was "discreet."[3]

In terms of available personnel, not much had changed from when the colonies had each formed their own militias. Rather than trained, disciplined, and seasoned soldiers, the troops under Washington's command were volunteers pulled from farm fields, clerking duties, shoeing horses, loading and unloading ships, and the like. What's more, they still seemed to think of themselves as belonging to their local militias instead of jelling as one centralized unit.

Causing more problems for General Washington was the fact that enlisted men were typically required to serve no more than six months at a time, a term that was later expanded to one year. According to Washington, even a year was not long enough to train an army properly.[4] In the beginning, it must have seemed to Washington as if he were losing men just as they were truly becoming decent soldiers.

The Battle of Bunker Hill

After his election, the commander in chief of the Continental Army got right to work. Knowing that British forces had gained a foothold in and around Boston since retreating there after the battles of Lexington and Concord,

This Currier and Ives lithograph depicts American "minute men" marching to the beat provided by a fife and drum. Militia soldiers like these were typically volunteers, not professional soldiers.

Washington set out for Massachusetts from Philadelphia immediately.

While he was on the move, an important battle was brewing in the hills overlooking Boston Harbor. Two days after Washington's election, American troops in Massachusetts found out that British troops were planning to take control of a hilly area overlooking Boston Harbor the following morning. Securing the area meant that British ships could safely enter the harbor to bring supplies to British regulars. To counter such a move, American forces marched to the area between Breed's Hill and Bunker Hill, and overnight they constructed a huge wall of fortified dirt designed to block the British advance up the hill to the high ground.

The British wound up winning the battle—but at a great cost. Nearly half of the more than two thousand British regulars who charged up Breed's Hill (where most of the fighting had occurred despite the historical name of the battle) lay dead or wounded after hours of fighting. The Americans had made a tremendous stand against a cocky foe, which encouraged them in their fight for independence.

The Attempt to Take Quebec

By the beginning of July, Washington had arrived in Cambridge, outside of Boston, which would become his military headquarters and the Continental Army training ground. Presumably stung by the British victory at Bunker Hill, he quickly proposed that the British be pushed out of Boston through a direct attack on the city. British forces had been stationed in the New England city since 1768. As far as the Americans were concerned, the continued presence of British regulars within the city constituted a standing army, meaning troops that were permanently encamped to enforce British rule rather than protect the populace.

Neither Congress nor Washington's fellow officers were keen on the idea. For one thing, they didn't think the American troops were ready for such a mission; they didn't want a resounding defeat to ruin the momentum built after the Americans' moral victory at Bunker Hill. So Washington shelved that plan, at least for the moment. Instead, he concentrated on gaining ground to the north in Canada.

At the end of August 1775, Continental Army forces under the command of General Richard Montgomery marched from Fort Ticonderoga, a formerly French-held and then British-held fort that had been overtaken by rebellion forces in May, along the St. Lawrence River and up toward Quebec. Along the way he captured a British fort and the Canadian city of Montreal. He had reached the outskirts of Quebec by the middle of November, and it was there that he awaited reinforcements from the Continental Army.

In September, Washington had ordered more than one thousand men, under the command of Colonel Benedict Arnold, to assume a position to the west of Quebec in order to surround the city on two sides. Those troops reconnoitered with Montgomery's men on December 2 after a tough march through the wilderness of Maine and western Canada in winter weather conditions.

Three days later, the attack on Quebec had begun in earnest. Unfortunately, a terrible snowstorm hit as the Continental troops began their advance on the city, which gave the British troops time to repel the attack. General Montgomery was killed on the first day, so Colonel Arnold assumed command of the remaining troops. Although they would fight for control of the city for several months, Arnold's forces were eventually forced to retreat. The campaign had been a resounding failure for the Americans.

Back to Boston

About the same time that the battle at Quebec was being waged—and lost—Washington ordered Major General Henry Knox to travel to Fort Ticonderoga and retrieve the artillery that the British had abandoned there. Knox and his

On an Eighty-Ox Open Sleigh

Henry Knox's weapons retrieval mission to Fort Ticonderoga could not have occurred at a worse time. Under the best of conditions, transporting artillery weighing thousands of pounds from northern New York to Cambridge would have been no small feat, albeit doable. However, Knox and his men were sent just as winter weather was settling into the area. In fact, the company was plagued by snow and cold breezes by the time it reached the fort, which threatened the timely delivery of the cannons.

Unable to simply roll the heavy guns on wheeled caissons, which is how cannons are typically maneuvered, through the drifting snow, Knox ordered his men to build forty-two sleds that could handle the load. Each sled was yoked to two oxen, which pulled the cannons through the worst of the terrain all the way to Springfield, Massachusetts. From there, the guns were delivered by cattle to Cambridge.

It is interesting to note that, in a letter to Washington describing the particulars of his journey dated December 17, Knox mentions the Quebec campaign: "… by the different accounts which I have been able to collect I have very little doubt that General Montgomery has Quebec in his possession."[6]

squad delivered more than fifty cannons, including howitzers and mortars, to Washington by the end of January 1776.[5]

On the evening of March 4, Washington had his troops in Cambridge fire on the British encampments throughout the night. The British were so busy returning fire they never saw the other American troops pulling several of the Ticonderoga cannons up to a hilly area of south Boston called Dorchester Heights. From there, the Americans had a clear view of, and a straight shot into, the heart of the city.

❝My God, these fellows have done more work in one night than I could make my army do in three months.❞

—Attributed to General William Howe

With their defeat following the Siege of Boston, British troops, along with Boston colonists loyal to the Crown, sailed out of Boston Harbor bound for Canada.

The British were caught completely off guard by the sight of the Americans and their artillery the next morning. British Commander General William Howe ordered his men to march up into the hills to engage the Americans, but once again Mother Nature interfered; the British advance was halted before it really got started by a blinding snowstorm. Feeling outgunned and out maneuvered, Howe ordered a withdrawal of British troops from Boston. Reportedly hundreds of loyalists, meaning colonists loyal to the Crown, sailed out of Boston Harbor on March 17, 1776, bound for Nova Scotia in the Canadian territories. It had taken longer than he expected or hoped, but Washington had finally ended the years-long occupation of the city by opposing forces.

Declaring Independence and War

The day after the British left Boston, Washington took a brief victory lap around the city before getting back down to business. Having been flushed out of Boston, the British were bound to go looking for another strategic location in which to establish their presence in the colonies. Washington suspected they might try to get a foothold in New York City because that area would give them easy access to British strongholds in Canada.

In late June 1776, a fleet of British ships was spotted sailing from Nova Scotia in the direction of New York. Washington sent word that the Massachusetts militia should make its way to the city as quickly as possible; then he set out for New York in anticipation of new battles with the British on American soil.

Benjamin Franklin, Samuel Adams, and Thomas Jefferson (*left to right*) hashing out a draft of the Declaration of Independence in Philadelphia.

Less than a week later, Congress met again in Philadelphia, and on July 2, the assembled body voted to officially declare America's independence from Britain. To seal the deal, they adopted the Declaration of Independence on July 4, 1776, the writing of which had been led by Thomas Jefferson.

As commander of the American armed forces, George Washington received a copy of the Declaration five days later in New York. In front of the assembled troops, he made a short speech of his own to announce that Congress had made America a union of "free and independent states" before launching into a recitation of the stirring words that spelled out for King George III that the thirteen colonies should now be considered a unified nation.[7]

WIN SOME, LOSE SOME

The response from his troops to the reading of the Declaration of Independence must have been gratifying for Washington. But any sense of satisfaction he might have felt was most likely short-lived. Although a formality at that point, given the fighting that had occurred over the previous two years, declaring the colonies' break from Britain was bound to anger the Crown into stepping up its assaults. Indeed, several of His Majesty's ships had delivered tens of thousands of troops to New York City's shores at Staten Island, along with thousands more Hessian, or German, soldiers hired to fight on the side of Britain. This gathering of enemy forces was the very reason Washington was in New York in the first place. There was no time for prolonged celebration. The commander and his troops had work to do.

> 66 The fate of unborn millions will now depend, under God, on the courage and conduct of this army. 99

The Battle of Long Island

Washington's army in New York was encamped on the western end of Long Island in Brooklyn Heights, across the East River from Staten Island. Troops were stationed to the south and southwest of the army's position. As mentioned, British and Hessian troops had occupied Staten Island. The American troops were outmanned, certainly in number but also in capability, given the short enlistment time and wavering ability and desire to fight on the part of Continental soldiers.

Historian Joe Ellis makes the interesting point that immediately prior to the campaign on Long Island, neither side sought the complete annihilation of the other. General William Howe and his admiral brother Richard were convinced that by handing the Continental Army a few hard defeats they could get the Americans to realize their effort for independence was futile. In other words, the Howes were ready to negotiate an end to the hostilities and bring the colonies "back into the fold." In fact, William Howe reportedly offered Washington and his troops a pardon for their rebellious ways shortly after both sides were stationed in their respective positions in New York. (Washington, of course, refused the offer.)[1]

For his part, Ellis has contended, Washington reasoned that even if he could not defeat the British outright on Long Island, at least his troops could inflict enough damage that the British would be humiliated and demoralized, making it harder for them to win other battles.[2] As it turns out, he could not have been more wrong.

On August 27, the British marched up through the Jamaica Pass—the one side of the Continental Army's

Portrait of General William Howe by artist Richard Purcell. Howe was part nemesis, part worthy opponent to Washington during the American Revolution.

perimeter that, for some unknown reason, was virtually unguarded—and surrounded the American troops at Brooklyn Heights. The Americans put up a good fight, but in the end they were no match for the British-Hessian

"War of Posts"

One good thing did come of the Continental Army's defeat on Long Island. Recognizing that he was too frequently going to be outmanned, outgunned, and outclassed by the British regulars, Washington devised a strategy for winning the war that depended on being a nuisance rather than a fierce warrior. The strategy, which Washington called a "war of posts" in a letter to Congress shortly after the Long Island battle, was borrowed, knowingly or unknowingly, from the ancient Roman Emperor Fabius Maximus. In his letter, Washington promised himself and Congress that he would not take any risks in battle "unless compelled by a necessity, into which we ought never to be drawn."[3] Rather than engage in direct attacks, where Continental troops risked being trapped and slaughtered, the "war of posts" called for the Americans to engage in sneak attacks and several smaller skirmishes with an escape route at the ready. The hope was to draw out the war long enough that the British would tire and give up or time (and, perhaps, friendly French allies) would turn the tide of the war in the Americans' favor.

tag team. Washington ordered a retreat on August 29 and crossed the East River for refuge on Manhattan Island.

Elsewhere in New York

After the retreat during the Battle of Long Island, George Washington directed his men north to Harlem Heights. While encamped there in September, the Continental Army again found themselves under attack from British forces, led by General William Howe, marching up from Staten Island and lower Manhattan. Washington sent a portion of his troops to confront the British head-on, but he also ordered four companies of men to skirt to the side of the British line and come up behind the enemy. It is unfortunate that the officers leading the flank attack turned too soon and wound up meeting British troops face to face instead of sneaking up behind them. However, it seems as though the intended maneuver spooked the British officers because after a brief battle they sounded the retreat from Harlem Heights. The Continental Army had held its ground.

A month later, the British were attacking again by staging a campaign in which foot soldiers were to be taken up the East River by boat and land at Throgs Neck, which was behind the American position in upper Manhattan. The Americans were able to block the British ships temporarily, which gave General Washington enough time to move his troops northward out of Manhattan and into Westchester County. There he hoped to put off the enemy long enough to gather supplies at a depot in White Plains and retreat farther north.

It quickly became apparent, however, that Howe's men would make it to White Plains before the Americans could retreat, so Washington began to position his troops in anticipation of battle. On the morning of October 28, 1776, British and German troops marched on the American line near an area called Chatterton's Hill. There the Continental Army dug in, literally, as Washington had commanded his corps of engineers to dig trenches in front of the hill.

British troops came straight at the Americans with cannons booming while their German allies attacked from

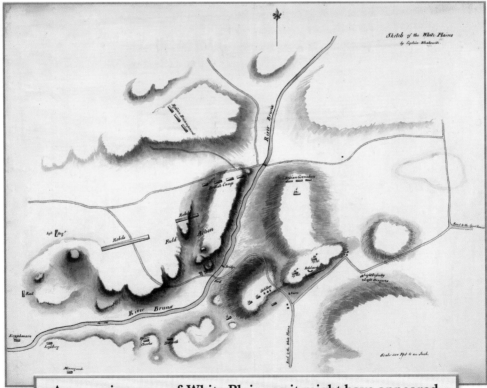

An overview map of White Plains as it might have appeared in 1776. The Battle of White Plains forced Washington and his troops out of New York City completely.

the right on horseback. After three days of intense fighting, Washington sensed that his troops were in danger of being trapped. He ordered the men to retreat farther northward on November 1. By the end of that month, General Howe's men had not only captured Forts Washington and Lee, on the Hudson River, but they had also pushed American forces out of New York completely. With British troops in hot pursuit, Washington moved his forces through neighboring New Jersey and finally settled in Pennsylvania in early December. Due to the close proximity of British forces and battle lines, should fighting erupt again, the members of Congress temporarily relocated to Baltimore, Maryland.

A Chance at Redemption

By the time the American troops had reached Pennsylvania, both sides were ready for the traditional winter encampment, wherein military activity almost ceased until the spring thaw when weather was more conducive to battle. A few companies of General Howe's men made camp in New Jersey, largely in and around Trenton and Princeton. The Continental Army, meanwhile, roughed it along the banks of the Delaware River in Pennsylvania.

But Washington wasn't content to simply wait out the weather. His army had suffered numerous defeats over the course of the fall, and the effect was a severe drop in reenlistments and a rise in desertions. In short, his forces were falling apart and in desperate need of a victory. So he decided to do the unexpected—cross back over the Delaware and attack opposing forces at Trenton in the dead of winter.

Emanuel Leutze's famous painting titled *Washington Crossing the Delaware.* **The artist ably captures the miserable winter conditions faced by General Washington and the Continental Army during the crossing.**

On Christmas night, the plan he had hatched was put into action. Blinding snow had kept full companies from reaching their departure points along the banks of the river on time, and the blizzard stirred up raging currents that stalled the actual crossing. Still, in miserable weather featuring ice- and slush-clogged waters and winds that pelted sleet in their faces, Washington and nearly 2,500 of his men quietly yet steadfastly rowed across to the far shore while ferrying large pieces of artillery, as well. Then they marched ten miles to the Hessian-controlled city.

Washington's gamble was successful. Early on the morning of December 26, American troops first overtook a company of German soldiers standing guard outside Trenton and then marched, artillery and guns resounding,

A Picture-Perfect Crossing

The trip across the Delaware on that stormy winter night was pretty ugly. Yet thanks to a nineteenth-century artist named Emanuel Gottlieb Leutze, the crossing turned out to be pretty as a picture.

Leutze's simply titled *Washington Crossing the Delaware* has its own battle story to tell. The original version of the painting was damaged in a fire at the artist's studio. Leutze was able to restore the work, which was purchased in the 1850s and put on display in a German museum. Nearly a century later, during a World War II bombing raid on Germany, the painting was destroyed. Luckily, Leutze had painted a replica shortly after the fire. That copy hangs in New York City's Metropolitan Museum of Art, which purchased the replica in 1897.[4]

into the city itself. They overpowered the Hessians there, as well—no doubt helped by the fact that the Germans were still recuperating from their Christmas celebration, as some scholars have speculated. Their resolve strengthened by their victory in Trenton, the men of the Continental Army ventured back into New Jersey less than a week later and scored two victories against British troops outside of Trenton, along the Assunpink Creek and again in the town of Princeton.

Within ten days, the British and their German allies had lost an estimated two thousand soldiers while the

Americans lost about two hundred. Washington's strategy had worked, and the Americans enjoyed their first real taste of success in their battle for independence. Unfortunately, it would be a long time before General Washington and his men would be able to celebrate like this again.

VALLEY FORGE
TO VICTORY

After the successful campaign in New Jersey, the Continental Army was able to retain soldiers who, without a win, might very well have not re-upped their enlistment so they could go home to their families. Staying in their ranks was an artillery officer by the name of Alexander Hamilton. Upon the recommendation of General Nathanael Greene, Washington hired Hamilton to be his aide-de-camp in March 1777.

That month, a young aristocratic Frenchman, the Marquis de Lafayette, set sail bound for America and the chance to assist those fighting the British, who had killed his father in the French and Indian War. He received his Continental Army officer's commission on July 31 in Philadelphia. There, he met and immediately bonded with Washington, who later asked the nineteen-year-old to join his staff.

Following Trenton and Princeton, Washington gave his men a well-deserved rest when he decided to adhere to the

Portrait of Washington's friend, comrade, and confidante Gilbert du Motier, better known as the Marquis de Lafayette.

common tradition of maintaining a temporary ceasefire over the winter months. The troops of the Continental Army made winter camp in the mountains of New Jersey while the British under General William Howe remained in New York. In spring of that year, both armies began moving against each other once again.

The British had devised something of a two-pronged attack against Washington and his men. Lieutenant General John Burgoyne would march from Quebec into Albany and stage an attack to reclaim Fort Ticonderoga along the way. Howe and his troops would travel up the Hudson from New York and rendezvous with Burgoyne to stage a joint assault on New England.[1] Yet a sudden change of heart overtook Howe, who subsequently devised a campaign to capture the heart of the American rebellion, Philadelphia.

Through intelligence reports and by tracking Howe's progress up the Hudson by ship, Washington knew something was afoot but was not exactly sure what until Admiral Richard Howe's fleet was spotted in the Chesapeake Bay, south of Philadelphia. Howe's troops landed in northern Maryland on August 22, 1777, and were moving north by land through the first few days of September. Meanwhile, Washington's troops were moving across Pennsylvania and eventually set up camp near Chadds Ford along the Brandywine Creek.

The Battle of Brandywine

As Howe's men marched northward toward Philadelphia, they engaged in a handful of skirmishes with American advance troops, most notably at Cooch's Bridge in Delaware.

The Battle of Saratoga

Howe's decision to advance on Philadelphia wound up creating a world of trouble for one of his fellow British officers, General John Burgoyne. While Burgoyne was able to complete the first objective of his march on Albany, the capture of Fort Ticonderoga, the rest of his plan came apart. On September 19, the British engaged with recently fortified American troops, under the command of General Horatio Gates, at a location known as Freeman's Farm. That day, Burgoyne's men would hold their ground despite a fierce attack from the infantry led by Benedict Arnold. The British were not so fortunate a few days later, when they went on the offensive again. Without the support of Howe's forces, Burgoyne and his men were forced to retreat; the general surrendered ten days later on October 17.

The Battle of Saratoga would prove costly in other ways later in the war. The actions of Gates and Arnold caught the attention of the French, who had been watching their longtime adversary wage battle against its upstart colonies. Starting that month, France formally entered the war as an American ally.[2]

Artist's rendering of the wounded Lafayette being helped by an aide during the Battle of Brandywine, which took place on September 11, 1777.

On September 11, however, they came upon the real deal—the main thrust of the Continental Army stationed near the Brandywine.

Moving toward Philadelphia, Howe split his men into two divisions: one that was supposed to meet the Americans head-on and another that was ordered to flank them to the east. Washington had sent divisions to protect the eastern flank at what he considered its easiest access points. Howe's troops, however, found a spot that General Washington had not protected and crossed the creek without any interference.[3]

Troops under the command of a Hessian officer, Lieutenant Wilhelm von Knyphausen, were met by an ambush from the woods surrounding the main road to Chadds Ford. While inflicting some damage and a number of casualties on the British side, the Americans were eventually routed from the woods by von Knyphausen's men and forced to withdraw.

Farther north, the British flanking troops were making significant progress in approaching the rear of the Continental Army's battle line at Chadds Ford. Washington's men were able to counter the attack at first by firing on the enemy troops from positions on Birmingham Hill, but the British and their Hessian allies were able to take the hill before too long. Once the high ground of the hill was lost, the Americans put up resistance to the British advance, but the lines they formed were demolished quickly after they were established.

The Battle of Brandywine has been acknowledged as a major defeat for the rebels. Casualties on the American side numbered close to 1,100 killed, wounded, or captured. Still, Washington tried to put a good face on the situation. "Notwithstanding the misfortune of the day," he wrote in a letter to John Hancock, "I am happy to find the troops in good spirits; and I hope another time we shall compensate for the losses sustained."[4]

Historians have noted that the only thing that saved the Continental Army that day was its end, meaning the Americans were able to escape after the sun had set and the battlefield had gone dark. In the days after the battle, Howe advanced farther into Pennsylvania, and he captured Philadelphia on September 26, 1777.

Washington Strikes Back

Not one to take defeat lying down, Washington soon hatched a plan to take the fight to the British once more. The British had left a certain number of troops in and around Philadelphia, but Howe had moved a division of some nine thousand men to a camp in nearby Germantown. Knowing the American forces under his command outnumbered Howe's encamped men, Washington ordered an attack on Germantown early in the morning on October 4.

Things seemed to be going well for the Continental troops in the beginning. The Americans had marched successfully past soldiers on patrol, and some even made it into the British camp itself. But then things seemed to go wrong left and right—literally. Washington's plan to flank Howe's men from both sides of the camp went haywire, as they were not able to surround the Hessians to the right and troops mistimed their arrival on the left. Also, the weather was working against the Americans. The early morning fog was so dense that soldiers were having trouble getting their bearings, which caused a company under the command of General Sullivan to come under friendly fire, meaning their own men were shooting at them.

The chaos and disorganization gave Howe time to gather his troops and basically start fresh with a counterattack. When they realized that they were now being forced to go on the defensive—that the prey had become the hunter—the Americans retreated. The Germantown battle may have served as a statement to the British that the colonies were not giving up the fight, but it was hardly a success.

The Conway Cabal

Not even the future "father of his country" was immune to gossip, backbiting, and political maneuvering. In the fall of 1777, one of Washington's officers, Brigadier General Thomas Conway, had petitioned Congress for a promotion to major general based on his actions during the Battle of Brandywine, which he said far outshone those of his commander in chief. Washington vigorously blocked the promotion on the grounds that it would make Conway superior to many other officers who deserved to be promoted first, thereby putting a dent in troop morale. In response, Conway sent a letter to the Battle of Saratoga hero General Horatio Gates requesting that he offer to replace Washington as commander in chief of the Continental Army. Conway and Gates exchanged several letters tearing down Washington and his military skills. In one letter, Conway supposedly called Washington "a weak general."

Conway was not the only one grumbling about Washington. A group of congressmen, which included Samuel Adams, had jumped on the anti-Washington bandwagon and was working behind the scenes to try and

Portrait of Thomas Conway, the Continental Army general who led a movement to remove Washington from command of the American forces.

replace him. Together, the officers and congressmen created a cabal, or secret political faction.

The whole plot fell apart after Congress, while investigating the matter, demanded to see the "weak" letter, and neither Conway nor Gates could, or would, produce it. Additionally, several of Washington's other generals either spoke or wrote to Congress in support of their commander. The cabal was finished, and Washington remained in command of the army.[5]

Valley Forge

By December 1777, hostilities had temporarily ceased as the armies prepared to set up winter quarters. Washington and his men, who had been encamped in the hills not far from Philadelphia, set out to cross the Schuylkill River and take up temporary residence at Valley Forge. The trip took days longer than expected because of a snowstorm that swept through the area while the army was on the road. Adding to their troubles was the fact that food rations and supplies were very low, and many of the troops did not have adequate clothing or shoes.

Washington and his men had elected to move to the new camp location in part because there was a small village nearby, and supplies had been stored in the area. Unfortunately, the British had commandeered, or seized, the American goods shortly after the Battle of Brandywine, which left nothing for the Continental Army's arrival at Valley Forge on December 19. The village had been wiped off the map, as well.[6]

With empty stomachs, clothing in tatters, and their bare or exposed feet bleeding in the snow, the Americans set

Painting showing Washington (*second from left*) giving a soldier words of encouragement while American troops were encamped at Valley Forge.

about building log and stone huts to protect them from the cruel winter weather. These shelters were crude and not quite as effective against the elements as the stone house that Washington made his base of operations.

> **❝Naked and starving as they are we cannot enough admire the incomparable patience and fidelity of the soldiery...❞** [7]

A combination of poor nutrition and unhygienic living conditions at Valley Forge is thought to have opened the door to all types of illnesses and diseases. Many of the men suffered from dysentery, and typhus killed many soldiers. Smallpox, which Washington had contracted as a young man in Barbados, was another notorious threat. All told, the number of men lost to illness at Valley Forge in the winter of 1777 is estimated to have been upward of three thousand.

Snow and wind were a problem that winter, as was a hard, freezing rain that seemed to visit the camp daily. Horrible weather conditions not only made the men miserable but also hampered the arrival of supplies. In some places, roads and trails were covered in feet of snow, while in others they were layered with ice, which made bringing in supply wagons difficult, to say the least. Washington wrote to Congress repeatedly about the horrid conditions with requests for assistance, but he got little help.

A Draw at Monmouth

Things did not get better at Valley Forge until Spring 1778, when food and supplies were better able to reach the camp. Another hopeful event for the army was the arrival of French troops to join the fight against the British. French ships bearing several military regiments arrived at Valley Forge that spring to train with battered Continental troops, and more were promised in the near future.

The appearance of the French at the American camp certainly got the attention of the British troops, who had spent the winter in the relative luxury of Philadelphia. Wary of a confrontation with the French-fortified army, General Henry Clinton, who had taken over for General William Howe, ordered the evacuation of Philadelphia on June 18, 1778. The city was recaptured by the Americans without any fighting or casualties.

Washington was not content to merely let it go, however. He sent troops under the command of General Charles Lee to stall the retreating British troops as they marched toward New York City. Then Washington and the bulk of the army could catch up and engage the British in battle.

The American advance troops encountered the British in Monmouth, New Jersey. Unfortunately, Lee's tactics did not work as well as planned, and he ended up retreating and running smack-dab into his commander, as well as the reinforcements, outside the town's courthouse. After shaming Lee in front of all those assembled, Washington took charge of the combined American forces and led them back to fight the British at Monmouth.

The fighting lasted into the evening, when Washington decided he would wait until morning and start anew. Overnight, the British managed to slip away and continue their march toward New York. The Battle of Monmouth had ended with nearly the same number of casualties on each side and no definitive winner or loser.

Changing Fortunes at Yorktown

For the next three years, the bulk of fighting in the Revolutionary War took place in the South, particularly in South Carolina and Georgia. Washington commanded his troops from his position in the North by entrusting them to handpicked generals and other officers. Even with the sworn aid of the French, the Americans suffered several defeats in the South. The situation looked bleak for the cause of independence.

But when Washington named General Nathanael Greene commander of the Southern Army, things began to turn around. Greene and his men scored a number of victories in South Carolina, much to the annoyance of General Charles Cornwallis, the British second in command under Clinton. Frustrated by Greene's maneuvers and battlefield wins, Cornwallis decided to

British troops surrendered to George Washington at Yorktown. Some historians report that General Cornwallis avoided the ceremony and had another officer present Washington with his sword.

move the fight to Washington's home territory, Virginia. They arrived in Petersburg on May 20, 1781. Cornwallis moved his base of command to nearby Yorktown.

Meanwhile, at the urging of French General de Rochambeau, Washington decided to march his troops down to Virginia, where they would meet with a French naval fleet sailing up the coast from the Caribbean into Chesapeake Bay. In order to escape undetected and therefore unharrassed by Clinton's troops, he planted a story about an American attack on New York City. He even went so far as to construct fake encampments as a diversion. The trick worked. Washington, de Rochambeau, and their troops began their march to Virginia.

The French ships, which had arrived in the bay in August, were met by a smaller British fleet a few weeks later on September 5. A naval battle ensued with the French and their superior numbers winning the day. With the French firmly in control of the bay, Cornwallis's escape route from Yorktown was blocked. Washington's troops arrived in the area in September; by October 3, Yorktown was completely surrounded by land and by sea. The Americans and French inched ever closer to Cornwallis's position in the town by building long trenches that they filled with men and artillery. They bombarded the town mercilessly. Seeing no way out, Cornwallis surrendered at Yorktown on October 19, 1781.

Following the surrender, the Americans held eight thousand troops as prisoners and took nearly as many guns and artillery units from the British. Tired, humiliated, and with waning support from citizens back home, the British decided to call an end to hostilities. In October 1783, the Treaty of Paris officially ended the Revolutionary War.

PRESIDENT WASHINGTON

With the signing of the Treaty of Paris in 1783, America's war for independence came to a close. So, too, had the military career of General George Washington. About a month after the treaty was signed, Washington resigned as commander of the Continental Army. Ever an honorable leader, in his resignation speech before Congress he made sure to mention the officers under his command and what was due to them in return for their service:

> While I repeat my obligations to the Army in general, I should do injustice to my own feelings not to acknowledge in this place the peculiar Services and distinguished merits of the Gentlemen who have been attached to my person during the War. It was impossible the choice of confidential Officers to compose my family should have been more fortunate. Permit me Sir, to recommend in particular those, who have continued in Service to the present moment, as worthy of the favorable notice and patronage of Congress.[1]

General George Washington Resigning His Commission by John Trumbull. This would be the third, and final, time that Washington would offer his military resignation.

Washington was content to simply go back home, to Martha and Mount Vernon, and once again try his hand at being a gentleman farmer. He was curious about new methods of planting and yield. After consulting with several British agriculturists, he decided to rework the fields on all his farms and incorporate a system of crop rotation to keep the soil from losing too many nutrients. The life of a farmer suited him. As he wrote in a letter to the Marquis de Lafayette, "I have become a private citizen on the banks of the Potomac, and under the shadow of my own vine and my own fig tree … I will move gently down the stream of life until I sleep with my fathers."[2]

Fortunately for the citizens of the United States, Washington would not make good on his promise to remain in retirement for the rest of his days.

The Constitutional Convention

On July 12, 1776, Congress drafted the Articles of Confederation, an agreement among the thirteen colonies regarding how they would work together as a unified whole, called the United States of America. The Articles, which the states did not officially ratify until 1781, were a nice wartime guideline on how the newly formed government should work. Once the war was over, however, the unity among separate states, which were used to running their own independent governments and militias, was put to the test. Disputes over land claims and issues surrounding trade and taxation led to a call for a Constitutional Convention.

The goal of the convention was to sculpt a constitution for the new nation that would replace the Articles of Confederation. Washington was named a convention delegate from Virginia. He made his way to Philadelphia's Independence Hall for the start of the proceedings in May 1787. Presumably based on his military service and the fact that he had been a delegate to both the First and Second Continental Congress, he was elected president of the Convention. As such, he oversaw debates between congressmen and helped guide the legislature in the drafting of the US Constitution.

Although he tried to remain impartial during the proceedings, Washington was a backer of the Virginia Plan, which proposed a federal government divided into three branches and a built-in system of checks and balances. The

George Washington (*standing on the right*) presiding over the signing of the US Constitution in 1787. This historic painting, by Howard Chandler Christy, hangs in the US Capitol Building.

plan also called for larger states with greater populations to have greater representation in Congress—versus the "one state, one vote" policy of the rival New Jersey Plan, which also favored a one-house legislature and less power overall to the central government.

In the end, the framers of the Constitution reached a compromise. The United States would have a two-house legislature with the Senate and the House of Representatives. Each state would have an equal number of representatives in the Senate, but a number proportional to its size and population in the House.

Leadership of the New Nation

Once the Constitution was ratified by a majority of states the following summer, Congress set about forming a centralized government—a concept that Washington favored. Congress determined that a body of electors should be chosen from each state that had ratified the Constitution (North Carolina and Rhode Island had yet to do so) so they could cast a representative vote from their state for a single leader of the new government. The electors overwhelmingly chose George Washington to be the country's first governmental leader. On April 30, 1789, in the new capital of New York City, George Washington was sworn in as the first president of the United States of America.

Washington was keenly aware of the importance of the job he was about to undertake. Even though the Constitution offered guidelines regarding how the presidency should be run, he was, in effect, making it up as he went along. Congress and the citizenry of the country were keeping a close eye on him to make sure he did not suddenly get power hungry and pick up where King George III had left off prior to the war. Beyond that, he knew his actions and decisions would set a precedent not only for those who would be elected to the nation's highest office in the future but also for the way the entire US government was to be run for years, even centuries, to come.

❝Few who are not philosophical spectators can realize the difficult and delicate part which a man in my situation had to act ... I walk on untrodden ground.❞

Washington is being sworn in as the first president of the United States in New York City.

The Electoral College

Article II of the Constitution is the basis for what is known today as the Electoral College. Each state was given a specific number of electors based on the number of congressional delegates they had. States held the right to determine how their electors were chosen. Some had their state's legislature or governor appoint the electors, while others were chosen by voters in their state.

In 1789, electors were to cast one vote for president and another for vice president. The person receiving the most votes was elected president, while the person who received the next most was named vice president. By virtue of coming in second in 1789, John Adams was elected Washington's vice president.

One of Washington's first acts as president was to name advisors, or the heads of different governmental offices. When choosing the members of his cabinet, he made sure to select people who had both similar and opposing ideas so many schools of thought were represented during discussions and debates about important issues of the day. In addition to Vice President John Adams, Washington was served by a cabinet of four, including Thomas Jefferson, Alexander Hamilton, Henry Knox, and Edmund Randolph.

Washington's Cabinet

A fellow Virginian and member of the Second Continental Congress, Thomas Jefferson was appointed as secretary of state. He returned from his position in Paris as ambassador to France to take his place in Washington's cabinet. Unlike others in Congress who, as Federalists, favored a strong federal government, Jefferson believed the nation's central government should have limited powers and give the individual states more of a say in governing themselves.

Portrait of Washington's first secretary of state, Thomas Jefferson. The portrait was painted by John Trumbull, who captured many historic American figures and moments on canvas.

Washington leaned toward a strong federal government, so it is quite probable that he added Jefferson to his cabinet to argue the merits of the other position.

Alexander Hamilton was the first cabinet member put before and approved by Congress. He had been Washington's aide-de-camp during the later years of the Revolutionary War, and therefore his views on a strong central government for the United States were well-known to the president. As secretary of the treasury, Hamilton was charged with overseeing the nation's economy and finding ways to reduce the national debt, which had skyrocketed over the course of the war. He is largely responsible for creating the First Bank of the United States.

Washington came to know and trust Henry Knox, who was appointed secretary of war, when he was a general during the war for independence. After retiring from military service in 1784, he was named secretary of war by Congress, a position he maintained into the Washington administration. Under Knox, the United States gained its navy and national army, which built off of Washington's Continental Army. The secretary also dealt with matters that cropped up with Native Americans on the western frontier. Knox favored respect for the natives regarding land rights and advised Washington on the president's handling of Indian affairs.

Edmund Randolph had served as an early aide for General Washington and as Virginia's attorney general and onetime governor. As governor, he was responsible for introducing the Virginia Plan during the Constitutional Convention. As the US attorney general, Randolph was tasked with forming the new nation's justice system.

Artist John Trumbull's portrait of Alexander Hamilton, who was appointed secretary of the treasury under President Washington.

John Jay was Washington's original choice for secretary of state, but he turned the job down. Instead, the president named him chief justice of the judicial branch of the federal government, the Supreme Court, which was formed when Washington signed into law the Judiciary Act of 1789. Although he was not part of the president's cabinet, Jay played an important role in the Washington administration.

Cabinet Conflicts

The president had gathered together advisors who had differing viewpoints, which had its advantages and disadvantages. On the positive side, Washington was able to see situations from many sides, which allowed him to make decisions that would be beneficial to the most people possible. On the downside, there could be heated disagreements among the cabinet members. Such was the case between two advisors in particular, Alexander Hamilton and Thomas Jefferson.

Hamilton's belief that the United States should have a strong federal government made him what people called a Federalist. Jefferson was decidedly an anti-Federalist, or in favor of giving individual states more power over how they governed themselves. The Federalists and the anti-Federalists, also called Republicans, were the first two political parties in the United States. Although Washington tried to stay impartial while listening to his advisors, he frequently sided with Hamilton on matters of policy. For instance, the president agreed with Hamilton's plans for the federal government to assume, or take on, the states' debt and to create a national bank, both of which Jefferson and the Republicans opposed. Further complicating the situation was the fact that both men, like the president himself, were finding their way when it came to what their newly created positions would entail. They frequently stepped on each other's toes—hard—when it came to whose job it was to decide policy on certain matters.[3]

The two did manage to come together and reach a very famous agreement called the Dinner Table Bargain. In 1790, Jefferson arranged to have his fellow Republican and influential congressman James Madison meet Hamilton for dinner in New York City. In a private dining room, the three men hammered out an agreement wherein Madison would help pass legislation establishing a national bank—something that Hamilton had been trying to accomplish for years—in exchange for Hamilton throwing his weight behind a plan to relocate the US capital to a site farther south on the Potomac River, which was a pet project of Madison and Jefferson.

Second Term

Most of Washington's first term as president was taken up with housekeeping matters, or issues of defining the nature of the job and then setting up the functions of the federal government. He must have done a good job because, once again, he was unanimously elected to the office in 1792. During his second term as president, Washington faced a number of political obstacles, both at home and abroad, that would test him as a politician and statesman.

One of the first involved a conflict between two familiar longtime rivals. In 1793, France declared war on Britain as a result of events surrounding the French Revolution

Stretching His Presidential Muscle

In 1792, Congress passed a bill that would presumably throw the power structure of the House of Representatives out of whack. The Constitution provided for the House to have a number of representatives proportional to its population. The Apportionment Bill sought to add one representative to each of the eight states whose overall population number did not divide evenly, which essentially, the bill's authors argued, left portions of each state without representation. But giving them an extra representative also gave those states an advantage when it came time to vote in the House.

After consulting with his cabinet, Washington decided to veto the bill on the grounds that it was unconstitutional. In doing so, the president was exercising a power granted to him by Article I, Section VII of the Constitution. Washington used his veto only once more during his two terms in office.

(1789–1799). With memories of the war for independence fresh in their minds, many Americans thought the United States should side with their former allies, the French. Others favored restoring relations with the British. George Washington chose to back neither side and took a neutral stance. He refused to have the United States enter another conflict while the new nation was trying to recover, financially and emotionally, from the Revolutionary War. Besides, little was to be gained by choosing one side over another in this battle between other nations.

Closer to home, in 1794 Washington faced a domestic crisis known as the Whiskey Rebellion. As a way to raise revenue, Hamilton had persuaded Congress to place a tax on the purchase of whiskey and other distilled spirits. Small farmers, who often used their grain crops to make alcohol for sale, felt that the tax was unfair and started to protest. When violence entered the picture, Washington first tried to negotiate with the rebels; then, when that failed, he called militia units from four states into action. Facing armed troops that numbered more than twenty times their own group of protestors, the rebels fled. Two of the rebellion's leaders, who had been caught and tried for treason, were later pardoned by the president.

Three years later, Washington again favored military action when there was trouble with Native American tribes on the western frontier in what is now Ohio. Settlers moving

A tax collector is tarred and feathered in response to the Whiskey Act of 1791. Washington sent in troops to break up the protests.

into the northwest territory were being attacked and killed by American Indians, who viewed the land as theirs. In response, Washington sent in a regiment of the United States Army, under the leadership of General Anthony Wayne, in August 1794. They were to engage warriors from a confederation of tribes. Known as the Battle of Fallen Timbers, the Native American confederation was defeated, and the United States negotiated a treaty with several of the tribes to move out of the area and agree not to attack American settlements again.[4]

The Jay Treaty

Also in 1794, relations with Britain were turning sour. The British were not abiding by all the conditions set forth in the Treaty of Paris. They were occupying certain forts on US soil and inciting Native Americans to stage attacks against American citizens. Furthermore, Britain was not respecting America's neutrality in their ongoing war with France—even going so far as turning away US ships loaded with goods from French ports, thereby restricting free trade. Tensions were high, and Washington and Congress feared that another war with Britain was imminent.

To defuse the situation, Washington sent Chief Justice John Jay to Britain to negotiate a treaty that would stop, or at least curb, hostilities between the two nations. Jay was not as successful as the Americans had hoped. Terms of the treaty definitely favored the British, who gave up very little in exchange for strict regulations governing American trade and ongoing relations with the French. Although he was displeased with the results, Washington urged Congress to ratify, or approve, the treaty, if only to keep the peace.

John Jay was Washington's chief justice, who negotiated a treaty with Britain that was not well received by the American public.

The president was not the only one disappointed with what became known as the Jay Treaty. Riots broke out across America when conditions of the agreement were made public. The unrest lasted for years with pockets of protest breaking out well into 1796—the year Washington left office.

A Fond Farewell

Infighting within his cabinet, rebellions, riots, and the ever-looming possibility of war with Britain, France, or both countries took their toll on the aging president. By the time his second term in office was up, Washington was more than ready to retreat back to Mount Vernon and restart the retirement that had been delayed for eight long years. He drafted a farewell speech, which he sent to Hamilton for review and editing. The end result wound up being printed in the newspaper instead of spoken.

Washington's farewell address was more than a retirement announcement or a summation of all he had accomplished in his years as president. His intent was to have future generations benefit from his experience, as well. Inspired by continued conflict between Federalists and Republicans, he stressed the need for unity above all else, writing, "The name of American, which belongs to you, in your national capacity, must always exalt the just pride of patriotism, more than any appellation derived from local distinctions."

Washington's farewell address proved that it could pass the test of time. From 1862 through the 1970s, the complete address was read each year in the chamber of the US Senate in late February to celebrate the former president's birthday.

CONCLUSION

As he had anticipated, Washington left a lasting impression on future generations through his actions as the first president of the United States. For instance, in choosing advisors who had contrary opinions on so many matters, he set in motion the birth of the two-party political system, which is a mainstay of American politics. He made being in office for only two terms the standard for US presidents, which is a circumstance that was made law in 1951. Overall, Washington established a number of firsts while in office that have resounded through the years and have now become the norm.

He also made his mark as a military commander. While he did not invent his "war of posts" strategy, Washington is credited for recognizing that he needed to adjust his battle plans and for adopting the strategy successfully. Moreover, he is noted for his spirit and determination, for attempting risky maneuvers on the battlefield, and for his willingness to wait out the enemy by keeping up the good fight.

Washington's legacy lives squarely in two worlds: military service and politics. More to the point, his accomplishments in both those arenas played a crucial role in making the United States of America the independent nation it is today.

CHRONOLOGY

Feb. 22, 1732

George Washington is born in Westmoreland County, Va.

1742

Father Augustine Washington dies

1748

Begins his first surveying journey into Northern Neck

1752

Brother Lawrence dies; appointed adjutant in the Va. militia

Dec. 1753

Allegheny Expedition; delivers ultimatum to the French (Fort LeBoeuf)

May 28, 1754

Jumonville Glen

July 3, 1754

Surrender at Fort Necessity

October 1754

Resigns his commission

July 9, 1755

Battle of Monongahela; Washington is Braddock's aide-de-camp; takes over when Braddock dies

May 1756

French and Indian War officially begins

1758

Resigns from the militia; marries Martha Dandridge Custis

April 1759

Attends first meeting as a Virginia House of Burgesses delegate

Sept. 4, 1774

First Continental Congress

May 10, 1775

Delegate to the Second Continental Congress

June 15, 1775

Appointed commander in chief of the Continental Army

July 3, 1775

Takes command of his troops

August 27, 1776

Battle of Long Island

Dec. 26, 1776

Crosses the Delaware; Battle of Trenton

Sept. 11, 1777

Battle of Brandywine

Oct. 4, 1777

Battle of Germantown

Dec. 19, 1777

Arrives at Valley Forge

June 28, 1778

Battle of Monmouth

Oct. 19, 1781

Victory at Yorktown; war concludes with the surrender of Cornwallis

Dec. 23, 1783

Surrenders commission for the third and final time

May 1787

Constitutional Convention

April 30, 1789

Inaugurated unanimously as first president in New York

1792

Unanimous reelection as president

1793

French declare war on Britain; Washington vows to remain neutral

Summer of 1794

Quells Whiskey Rebellion using armed forces

Aug. 18, 1795

Signs the Jay Treaty

Sept. 17, 1796

Farewell address published

Dec. 14, 1799

Dies at Mount Vernon

CHAPTER NOTES

CHAPTER 1 WHERE IT BEGAN

1. John Ferling, *The Ascent of George Washington* (New York, NY: Bloomsbury Press, 2009).
2. Staff, "Washington's Boyhood," The George Washington Foundation, November 2016, http://www.kenmore.org/ferryfarm/boyhood.html.
3. Kiera E. Nolan, "Lawrence Washington," George Washington's Mount Vernon, November 2016, http://www.mountvernon.org/digital-encyclopedia/article/lawrence-washington/.
4. Alicia K Anderson, "'The Epitome of Navigation': How Lawrence Washington Steered His Brother George," The Washington Papers website, http://gwpapers.virginia.edu/the-epitome-of-navigation-how-lawrence-washington-steered-his-brother-george/.
5. Saul K Padover, ed., *The Washington Papers* (New York, NY: Harper and Brothers, 1955).
6. Staff, "George Washington's Professional Surveys," Founders Online, November 2016, http://founders.archives.gov/documents/Washington/02-01-02-0004.
7. Jack Warren, "Journey to Barbados," George Washington's Mount Vernon, November 2016, http://www.mountvernon.org/george-washington/washingtons-youth/journey-to-barbados.
8. Staff, "The French and Indian War," George Washington's Mount Vernon, November 2016, http://www.mountvernon.org/george-washington/french-indian-war/.
9. Edward Eyres, "Militia in the Revolutionary War," American Revolution Museum at Yorktown, November 2016, http://www.historyisfun.org/yorktown-victory-center/militia-in-the-revolutionary-war/.

CHAPTER 2 A FIRST TASTE OF BATTLE

1. Saul K. Padover, ed., *The Washington Papers* (New York, NY: Harper and Brothers, 1955).

2. John Ferling, *The Ascent of George Washington* (New York, NY: Bloomsbury Press, 2009).

3. Padover, op. cit.

4. Ferling, op. cit.

5. Ferling, op. cit.

6. Joseph F. Stoltz, "The Jumonville Glen Skirmish," George Washington's Mount Vernon, November 2016, http://www. mountvernon.org/digital-encyclopedia/article/jumonville-glen-skirmish/.

7. Ibid.

8. Raymond Bial, *Where Washington Walked* (Markham, Ont.: Walker Publishing Company, 2004).

CHAPTER 3 AT WAR AND AT HOME

1. Staff, "Jumonville Glen," National Parks Service website, November 2016, https://www.nps.gov/fone/jumglen.htm.

2. John Ferling, *The Ascent of George Washington* (New York, NY: Bloomsbury Press, 2009).

3. Staff, "From George Washington to William Fairfax, 7 June 1755," Founders Online, November 2016, http://founders.archives.gov/?q=Volume%3AWashington-02-01&s=1511311112&r=155.

4. Milton Meltzer, *George Washington and the Birth of Our Nation* (New York, NY: Franklin Watts, 1986).

5. Staff, "The Battle of Monongahela," National Park Service, November 2016, https://www.nps.gov/fone/braddock.htm.

6. Staff, "Washington and the French & Indian War," George Washington's Mount Vernon, November 2016, http://www. mountvernon.org/george-washington/french-indian-war/washington-and-the-french-indian-war/.

7. W.W. Abbott and Dorothy Twohig, eds., *The Papers of George Washington, Colonial Series, Vol. 10* (Charlottesville, VA: University Press of Virginia, 1995).

8. "Washington and the French & Indian War," George Washington's Mount Vernon, op. cit.

CHAPTER 4 PRELUDE TO A REVOLUTION

1. Staff, "Farm Structure," The Digital Encyclopedia of George Washington, November 2016, http://www.mountvernon.org/digital-encyclopedia/article/farm-structure/.
2. Ibid.
3. Saul K. Padover, ed., *The Washington Papers* (New York, NY: Harper and Brothers, 1955).
4. Staff, "Family Life for the Washingtons," George Washington's Mount Vernon, November 2016, http://www.mountvernon.org/george-washington/martha-washington/family-life-for-the-washingtons/.
5. John Ferling, *The Ascent of George Washington*, (New York, NY: Bloomsbury Press, 2009).
6. Ibid.
7. Maria Kimberly, "House of Burgesses," The Digital Encyclopedia of George Washington, November 2016, http://www.mountvernon.org/digital-encyclopedia/article/house-of-burgesses/.
8. Milton Meltzer, *George Washington and the Birth of Our Nation* (London; Franklin Watts, 1986).
9. W.W. Abbott and Dorothy Twohig, eds. *The Papers of George Washington, Colonial Series, Vol. 10* (Charlottesville, VA: University Press of Virginia, 1995).

CHAPTER 5 THE BATTLE FOR INDEPENDENCE BEGINS

1. James MacDonald, "Appointment as Command in Chief," The Digital Encyclopedia of George Washington, November 2016, http://www.mountvernon.org/digital-encyclopedia/article/appointment-as-commander-in-chief/.

2. Benjamin L. Huggins, "George Washington Takes Command," The Papers of George Washington, November 2016, http://gwpapers.virginia.edu/george-washington-takes-command/.

3. John Ferling, *The Ascent of George Washington* (New York, NY: Bloomsbury Press, 2009).

4. Ibid.

5. Susan Ware, ed., *Forgotten Heroes: Inspiring American Portraits from Our Leading Historians* (New York, NY: Simon and Schuster, 1998).

6. Staff, "Dragging Cannon from Fort Ticonderoga to Boston, 1775," The Gilder Lehrman Institute of American History, November 2016, https://www.gilderlehrman.org/history-by-era/war-for-independence/resources/dragging-cannon-from-fort-ticonderoga-boston-1775.

7. Mary Stockwell, "Declaration of Independence," The Digital Encyclopedia of George Washington, December 2016, http://www.mountvernon.org/digital-encyclopedia/article/declaration-of-independence/.

CHAPTER 6 WIN SOME, LOSE SOME

1. Mary Stockwell, "Battle of Long Island," The Digital Encyclopedia of George Washington, December 2016, http://www.mountvernon.org/digital-encyclopedia/article/battle-of-long-island/.

2. Joe Ellis, "Washington and the New York Campaign of 1776," George Washington's Mount Vernon, Vimeo page, https://player.vimeo.com/video/68791191.

3. Staff, "Washington's Strategy: 'A War of Posts,'" Library of Congress, December 2016, http://www.loc.gov/teachers/classroommaterials/presentationsandactivities/presentations/timeline/amrev/north/posts.html.

4. Amanda Hamon, "Did you know: 'Washington Crossing the Delaware' painting," Purdue Today, February 2014, accessed December 2016, http://www.purdue.edu/newsroom/purdue

today/didyouknow/2014/Q1/did-you-know-washington-crossing-the-delaware-painting.html.

CHAPTER 7 VALLEY FORGE TO VICTORY

1. John Ferling, *The Ascent of George Washington* (New York, NY: Bloomsbury Press, 2009).
2. Thomas Fleming, "Battle of Saratoga," History.com, December 2016, http://www.history.com/topics/american-revolution/battle-of-saratoga.
3. Ferling, op. cit.
4. Staff, "Washington Describes the Battle at Brandywine Creek, September 11, 1777," Library of Congress, December 2016, http://www.loc.gov/teachers/classroommaterials/presentationsandactivities/presentations/timeline/amrev/turning/brandy.html.
5. Esther Pavao, "Conway Cabal," Revolutionary-War.net, accessed December 2016, http://www.revolutionary-war.net/conway-cabal.html.
6. Ron Avery, "The Story of Valley Forge," US History.org, accessed December 2016, http://www.ushistory.org/ValleyForge/history/vstory_background.html.
7. Stanley L. Klos, "Thomas Mifflin," The Forgotten Founding Fathers, accessed December 2106, http://theforgottenfounders.com/the-forgotten-fathers/thomas-mifflin/.

CHAPTER 8 PRESIDENT WASHINGTON

1. Staff, "George Washington resigns as commander in chief," History.com, accessed December 2016, http://www.history.com/this-day-in-history/george-washington-resigns-as-commander-in-chief.
2. Theodore J. Crackel, ed., "George Washington to Marquis de Lafayette, 1 February 1784," *The Papers of George Washington* (digital edition), Charlottesville, VA: University of Virginia Press, 2008.

3. Joanne B. Freeman, "Jefferson and Hamilton, Political Rivals in Washington's Cabinet," George Washington's Mount Vernon, accessed December 2016, http://www.mountvernon.org/george-washington/the-first-president/washingtons-presidential-cabinet/jefferson-and-hamilton-political-rivals/.

4. Peter Kotowski, "Whiskey Rebellion," The Digital Encyclopedia of George Washington, accessed December 2016, http://www.mountvernon.org/digital-encyclopedia/article/whiskey-rebellion/.

GLOSSARY

adjutant A military officer who assists a superior officer.

assiduously Done constantly and with great care.

barricade A physical barrier designed to keep the enemy from reaching a fighting force.

beleaguered The condition of being harassed or surrounded.

bureaucracy A policy-making group that performs largely administrative tasks.

burgess A British term meaning a representative of a town or borough.

commission A military position as an officer.

diplomatic A way of conducting business that is polite and does not offend anyone.

disarray Completely out of order and in a state of confusion.

disgruntled To be unhappy and upset.

flogged Beaten with a rod, stick, or whip.

lucrative Capable of making lots of money.

militia Armed forces made up of ordinary citizens rather than trained soldiers.

ratification To formally approve of something.

rations A portion of food allowed for one meal or one day.

reconnaissance A maneuver designed to gather information before taking action.

regiment A military unit.

repressive To put or keep down by using force.

skirmish A small armed battle.

surveyor One who measures and otherwise determines the size, shape, and location of land parcels.

trench A long, narrow ditch from which soldiers can fight or that is used to slow or stop the progress of the enemy.

FURTHER READING

BOOKS

Goddu, Krystyna Poray. *George Washington's Presidency*. Minneapolis, MN: Lerner Publications, 2017.

Palmer, David Richard. *George Washington's Military Genius*. Washington, DC: Regnery History, 2012.

Scudder, Horace E. *George Washington: An Historical Biography*. Boston, MA: Riverside Press, 2013.

Washington, George. *The Journal of Major George Washington, 1754*. Oxford, UK: Acheron Press, 2012.

WEBSITES

http://www.shmoop.com/george-washington/websites.html

http://millercenter.org/president/washington
https://www.whitehouse.gov/1600/presidents/georgewashington

FILMS

The Crossing
A&E Home Video, 2003

George Washington: The Complete Miniseries
CBS, 1984.

INDEX